Bootstrapped

I0471250

"How 75 Entrepreneurs Successfully Bootstrapped Their Startups and How You Can Too"

Copyright © 2013 James Garvin

ISBN: 978-1-48-419713-4

"Be the person that does it, not wishes it."
~James Garvin

Dedication

This book is dedicated to my son Bryce. Bryce, I started this book as a project when you were born in January of 2012. After 13 months of researching, writing, and editing, I have finally produced the following pages.

You inspired me to push forward and to ultimately finish what I started. You have taught me more lessons in our first year together than I could have imagined and I hope that this book reciprocates and teaches you some valuable life and business lessons one day.

My hope is that when you are ready, this book will provide you with the motivation and knowledge to go forward with your ideas and to ultimately follow your passions.

Never be afraid to go for it.

Love,

Dad

Table of Contents

About Bootstrapped

This book is about you!

It's about giving you the motivation and the guidance you need to start your own business without having to raise millions in venture capital. It's about giving you the confidence that you can succeed with your ideas by showing you how others, just like you, did it.

It's about showing you what business models have been proven successful by bootstrapping and to help you identify how to find your own ideas for a business.

I have researched thousands of startups. I'm intrigued to learn how they did it and more importantly, how more people like you can follow in their success. Bootstrapped shares the stories of a *carefully selected 75 startups and entrepreneurs* from a variety of industries and backgrounds.

While we often read about the Facebook's and Google's of the world, the vast majority (i.e. the 99+ %) of startups never raise any venture capital and yet they find ways to become profitable and succeed all the while getting to maintain complete control of their companies. Bootstrapped uncovers these hidden stories to show you that it's all possible.

The media and to an extent, our society, provide a false perception that in order to successfully start a business, you need to raise a lot of money. While this may be true for a small percentage of companies (i.e., the 1%) that require millions in startup capital to grow to $Billion companies, it is untrue for more than 99% of successful startups.

In Bootstrapped, you will learn not only how these savvy entrepreneurs bootstrapped their businesses, but you'll also learn how they came up with their ideas, the steps they took to transform their ideas into a business, and how they ultimately built and scaled their businesses to success.

Let's face it, most of us want to start our own business, but we often don't know where to start. In fact, just getting started is the BIGGEST reason why most of us never do it. And there are 2 false ideas that we give ourselves that are the cause of our inability to START something great:

1.) I don't have a good idea
2.) I don't have enough money

Bootstrapped will show you that finding a "good" business idea is a lot easier than you think AND that you often don't need a lot (if any) money to get started with your idea.

Who Are Bootstrappers?

For the most part, they are just like you and me. The MAJOR difference between successful Bootstrappers and you is this. **They take action with their ideas**. They don't over think, over analyze, or wait for the "perfect" time to bring their ideas to market.

There is a Japanese proverb that says *"A vision without action is just a daydream"*.

This is where most people fail. They never get started. They become paralyzed with fear of the unknown. They don't know how to get out of first gear. Bootstrappers know how to get from 1st gear to 5th gear using the most efficient means possible and the following stories will show you how they did it.

Where do their ideas come from? A lot of times they come by accident or they come from their own personal experiences to "scratch their own itch" or to solve a problem they personally experienced. They don't always set out to create multi-million dollar businesses. In fact, many started their businesses as a "side" project that over the years grew into a multi-million dollar business, but they were not planned that way.

What are their backgrounds? They come from a variety of backgrounds. Most entrepreneurs profiled in Bootstrapped have previously worked in the corporate world before setting their own sail. They are located all across the country from California to Michigan to Connecticut. Some have MBAs, others have little formal education. The diversity of successful entrepreneurs is the most uplifting to me because they are just like you and me. They don't have any magical super powers or advantages that you don't have yourself.

How do they pay the bills when starting? There are 4 primary ways Bootstrappers continue to pay the bills while building their startups:

1.) Maintain their full-time job and work on their startup part-time until they can earn enough on the side to comfortably leave their day jobs.
2.) They do consulting work on the side to bring in cash.
3.) They have saved enough cash and use their savings to pay their bills.
4.) They build a business that brings in cash very rapidly.

How much money do they start with? Bootstrappers started with as much as $500,000 scraped together from personal savings and family/friends and as little as $10 to purchase a domain name. "On average" Bootstrappers invest a few thousand dollars into their startups, but the amount of money is entirely dependent on the company, business model and the founder's skill sets.

Do they work alone or have partners? Both, but the majority have co-founders and for good reason. Co-founders often complement the skills of one another and allow them to work collectively to bootstrap a business. Many business entrepreneurs found technical programmers as co-founders and vice versa. The "big vision" entrepreneurs found tactical "detail-oriented" co-founders to help them execute on their ideas. However, there are several entrepreneurs who acted alone as sole founders of their companies and did equally well. The need for a co-founder is dependent on your personality, strengths, and cash availability.

How Have They Succeeded? None of the Bootstrappers in this book will tell you that their journey was easy. But that's what makes entrepreneurship so special. It's a feat accomplished by so few, not from the high number of failures, but from the high number that never try. Bootstrappers succeeded through years of sweat equity to build their businesses to where they are now. Many have even enjoyed successfully selling their businesses for tens of millions of dollars. Others are still building the startups they founded, but are reaping the rewards of knowing that they have crossed the chasm where most startups fail and on their way to a stable and thriving business.

A Thank You

To all the entrepreneurs who have made this book possible. Your stories inspire, motivate, and pave a path forward for aspiring entrepreneurs.

Also, a huge thank you to the resources I utilized in order to research and share the stories of the 75 startups. While some of the stories in Bootstrapped came from the founders themselves, many of the facts and figures used in the book came from secondary resources.

If you don't know of them already, the best online resources out there for researching startups and learning from entrepreneurs who have succeeded (and failed) are listed below by importance:

1.) Mixergy.com (Andrew Warner)
   a. By far the best resource to learn how entrepreneurs have succeeded (and failed). Andrew interviews startup founders and advisors on an almost daily basis. His interviews provide details about the startup process not found anywhere else and I highly recommend signing up for his premium entrepreneurship courses taught by entrepreneurs themselves.
2.) Entrepreneur blogs and company websites
3.) Inc.com
   a. An obvious choice, but they have great profiles and their Inc. 5000 list is superb.
4.) Entrepreneur.com
   a. Another obvious choice, but they do great interviews with startup founders who share valuable insights on their experiences.
5.) Techcrunch.com
   a. While they focus more on VC backed startups, this is the go to place for internet startup news and events and occasionally provide exclusive stories on bootstrapped startups and entrepreneurs.

Online Media

"One of the most common causes of failure is the habit of quitting when one is overtaken by temporary defeat." ~ *Napoleon Hill*

Climbing the Marketing Mountain, One Member at a Time

Company: Marketing Sherpa
Website: www.marketingsherpa.com
Last Known Revenue: Undisclosed

Who Are They? Marketing Sherpa is the guide you've been looking for on your trek up Marketing Mountain. A sherpa knows the lay of the land. He lets you know not to step on what looks like solid ground but isn't. He shows you the best path to the summit. And a really good sherpa carries a "backpack" full of useful stuff. That's where Marketing Sherpa comes in: they give you the "backpack" for your own use!

How They're Doing It: A membership site over 300,000 strong, for one thing—that eventually earned Marketing Sherpa (backpack and all) a new mountaintop chalet of its very own, thanks to MarketingExperiments.com, who bought it for *millions* (with an "s") of dollars! [1]

Where They Came From: Anne Holland (@AnneHolland55) had been in publishing a long time, doing what people in publishing do: looking for ways to "get the word out" about their enterprises. One fateful day in 1999, as she climbed the various mountains of marketing conferences, networking, and trade shows (yeah, it's a metaphor; humor us here), she kept hearing the same calls for help: "We all know the theories. We all know the principles. We all know the processes. But doesn't anyone know of actual real, live *people* who've used them and made them work?"

"Of course, we do," Anne thought. "So why don't we *all* know about them?" Perhaps because no one had collected those success stories and case histories to share? *Voilá!* Marketing Sherpa was born: the place all those mountain-climbers could go to get the goods on all things marketing. [1]

What They Did Next: Even sherpas can find more challenging mountains, and so did Marketing Sherpa.

---

[1] http://mixergy.com/anne-holland-whichtestwon-interview/

Anne's endeavors (with a little help from the great influx of cash!) spawned a new venture, SubscriptionSiteInsider.com, just packed (there's that backpack again) with great ideas on everything from making your OWN membership site work to streamlining your billing...and knowing when NOT billing anything for content can pay off handsomely in the end.

The End Result? Marketers of all mountain-climbing skill levels can move from the area of "rocks and boulders"—a less-than-stellar membership site—to one that runs smoothly and well. The ingredients are simple: predictable, recurring revenue, plus content that scales, and testing...testing...and more testing. Anne is such a fan of A/B testing that she's put up its very own site: www.whichtestwon.com—so you can see the tests that lead to the most conversions!

"All Things Facebook"— Glittering like Gold!

Company: All Facebook
Website: www.allfacebook.com
Last Known Revenue: $250,000[2]

Who They Are: AllFacebook.com is a company in a unique position—the "unofficial" Facebook resource. If you want coverage on "everything Facebook," including everyone who uses it...this blog and news resource is your place to go for advice, news, and analysis.

How They're Doing It: Quite simply, they're trading off the "Facebook fascination" so many of us have. According to Compete.com, AllFacebook.com receives ~200,000 unique visitors per month—people interested in finding out what Facebook's doing, where they are, and what they're up to next...primarily supported by online display ads.

Where They Came From: AllFacebook.com was the brainchild of Nick O'Neill (@allnick), who launched it in May 2007, after Facebook launched their platform. At the time Nick, who was writing a blog called "Webpreneur," started thinking about the possibilities Facebook would present in the near future. With its rapid growth and soaring popularity, he figured it was certainly worth well blogging about; from there, it wasn't a long step to Nick's decision to build a "go-to" place for people who wanted to both understand Facebook and follow its development as an up-and-coming business phenomenon. [2]

Initially funded with a loan from his uncle and a $30,000 line of credit[2], AllFacebook began as a Wordpress-based blog, which Nick worked with to customize; sounds complicated, but Nick asserts the whole thing took under 12 hours to set up and launch. [2] It's focus? Not hard news or dry tech stories, but personal stories of those connected to Facebook instead. Making stories personal makes them easy to "connect" with—and a better read. [2]

---

[2] http://mixergy.com/nick-oneill-allfacebook-interview/

Not all those "personal" connections worked well, however: podcasts and "street interviews," two early experiments Nick tried to enhance the content, failed miserably. But sometimes the essence of entrepreneurship—and the ultimate secret to its success—is that willingness to try new things and fall on one's face. He didn't stay down long; the unique approach Nick has taken to becoming the "all things Facebook" source has earned him a loyal following...and a substantial nest egg of cash, to boot.

How substantial? Well, the fascination with Facebook and blogging about it paid off, in less than two years, when Nick sold AllFacebook to WebMediaBrand for "somewhere north of a million dollars." [2] Not bad for a site that, at the time of its sale, was listed as having about $250,000 in revenue!

The experts are right: social media pays off. For AllFacebook's founder, it's paid off big-time.

Getting the Story Out

Company: Help a Reporter Out
Website: www.helpareporter.com
Last Known Revenue: >$1 Million[3]

Who They Are: HARO (Help a Reporter Out) is a company providing source material for journalists everywhere. From its humble start as a Facebook app, HARO has become the go-to place for interviews, story ideas, and connections.

How They're Doing It: Three times a day, five days a week, the folks at HARO send e-mails out chock-full of media inquiries—to a mailing list of over 100,000 readers. As a virtual "matchmaker" for authors and content, HARO brings together nearly 30,000 reporters and bloggers, over 100,000 news sources, and thousands of small businesses to tell their stories and share their expertise and opinions. [4] In short, it's both a networking opportunity and an information "motherlode."

And...all this wonderful stuff is FREE. That's because, unlike so many social media services, HARO is independently owned and funded. Also unlike so many startups, HARO has been profitable from the first day. Where does the money come from? As a wizened veteran might put it, "Advertisin', my boy, advertisin'!" With text-based ads at the top of every single one of those 15 weekly e-mails, the ad revenue has added up fast—to the tune of seven figures.

Where They Came From: Finding the right people, the verifiable information, and the best sources—on deadline— is a constant challenge for journalists. Peter Shankman (@petershankman), a PR pro, encountered these needs every day. So, in 2008, he decided to "help a reporter out," primarily reporters who were his personal friends and contacts. The rest has been profitable history...all the way to HARO's acquisition by Vocus in 2010[5], enabling

---

[3] http://mixergy.com/haro-peter-shankman/
[4] http://www.vocus.com/blog/our-new-haro-publicity-alerts-are-live-choose-your-package/
[5] http://www.bizjournals.com/washington/stories/2010/06/07/daily47.html

Shankman to gracefully step away from the project and pursue other ventures.

Most gratifying for Shankman, however, isn't the Vocus purchase so much as what he's been able to do for the people he started out serving in the first place. "There have been stories covering enterprises and people who had to potentially shut down their businesses," he says. "[But] They were able to save their business because of the media experience they had. That's really exciting."[6]

That's serendipity and entrepreneurship at its best: starting out to help one group and having a ripple effect much further afield. For many businesses, as it turns out, "gold" is actually spelled H-A-R-O!

---

[6] http://www.socialmediaexaminer.com/how-help-a-reporter-out-grew-to-a-mega-network/

The "Little Blog That Could"—$30 Million Strong

Company: TechCrunch
Website: www.techcrunch.com
Last Known Revenue: Estimated at $6-$8 Million (2010)[7]

Who Are They? TechCrunch is your leading Internet tech media company; you want the latest scoop on startups, they're "who you're gonna call." From its beginnings as one man's tech blog, TechCrunch has grown to reach an audience of over 12 million unique visitors and 37 million page views per month.[8]

How They're Doing It: Two ways — primarily, through online ads; secondarily, through annual conferences. Oh, and now...the $30 million sale to AOL in 2010[9] (as part of America Online's expansion into online media companies) doesn't hurt, either.

Where They Came From: Once upon a time (along about 2005), Michael Arrington (@arrington) was a Silicon Valley attorney whose interest in new technology and new companies prompted him to start a blog about startup companies and Internet products. At that point, Arrington *was* "TechCrunch." He did the lion's share of blogging himself for its entire first year.

Then...something happened.

People started talking about TechCrunch. People liked Arrington's approach. They wanted more of his expertise. Arrington wrote more, people buzzed more, and before he knew it, Arrington's worldwide audience turned his humble blog into a full-time job.[10]

TechCrunch isn't just Arrington's baby anymore, either. Like any precocious kid, it grew fast and smart, and quickly became the place to go for breaking news in Silicon Valley. It covers all the bases from venture funding to acquisitions

---

[7] http://blogs.wsj.com/deals/2010/09/28/exactly-what-is-techcrunch-worth/
[8] Techcrunch.com
[9] http://online.wsj.com/article/SB10001424052748703882404575519831320838198.html
[10] http://www.webhostingreport.com/learn/techcrunch.html

to "what's hot on the street" — so well, in fact, that TechCrunch actually helps launch new ventures now.

Startups that want media attention give TechCrunch an exclusive scoop on their breaking story and, in return, they get spotlighted by the #1 source for technology and Internet startup news.

Being "first on the block" with information no one else does quite the same way has made TechCrunch the "go-to" source for hot Internet and technology news — which is no doubt why AOL decided that, at a cool $30 million, they'd be a bargain indeed!

Online Financial Wisdom "By the Slice"

Company: Killer Aces Media (Wisebread.com)
Website: www.wisebread.com
Last Known Revenue: ~ $1 Million

Who They Are: Killer Aces Media is a network of community blogs including one of the most popular personal finance blogs, wisebread.com. Their blog network reaches millions of readers a year, spanning 187 countries around the world.

How They're Doing It: Killer Aces generates revenue via online advertising it sells through its network partner, Federated Media, an ad agency started by John Battelle (who also helped launch Wired and The Industry Standard). The CPM (cost per thousand page views) ranges from $17 to $21 for its wisebread.com site—which averages 2.2 million page views each month.

Where They Came From: Friendship played a large role in the enterprise; the three Wise Bread cofounders have been great friends since high school. When they hit their respective strides as businesspeople, however, they saw an unfilled need—at least unfilled in any way that resonated with them and their peers. As founder Will Chen explains:

"We started Wise Bread in 2006 to learn more about personal finance. At the time I was a young attorney, Greg was a tech guru for an Academy Award-winning special-effects firm, and Lynn worked at King World Productions, which handled advertising for CBS and The Oprah Winfrey Show. We had decent salaries but didn't know how to save any of it. We looked for help online, but most personal finance resources didn't connect with us. That's when we decided to start a blog that would cover personal finance in a fun and appealing way."

Wise Bread lived up to its name from the start: it cost the founders almost nothing to begin, except maybe $8 to register the domain. They immediately recruited a lot of great writers, and before they knew it, their content was consistently hitting the front pages of Digg, Reddit, Boing Boing, Lifehacker, and the Consumerist. That's when they knew they had struck a nerve—in a good way!

Wise Bread's profitability increased dramatically in 2007 when they joined Federated Media. FM, in turn, gained Wise Bread national advertising campaigns with big brands like American Express, Intuit, Microsoft, Intel, Comcast, and HP.

How do they keep doing it so well? Attention to detail, as Chen explains. "The key to our success is our obsessive devotion to creating templates," he says. "We spend countless hours developing processes and instructions for our coworkers. This frees up the cofounders to focus on high-level strategies. Developing templates is tedious, mind-numbing work. But it is the most important thing you can do as a business owner if you want to succeed."

Wise Bread's "wisdom" has proven this true, over and over again— with the result that this "frugal living" site is enabling its founders and writers to live very profitably, indeed.

People, Places, Trends...and Video

Company: Mojo Supreme (WatchMojo)
Website: www.watchmojo.com
Last Known Revenue: Undisclosed

Who They Are: WatchMojo is a company full of people who are passionate about lots of subjects—from cars to business, education to fashion and film, food and travel to health, science, and parenting issues, politics and economics to sports and video games—and who produce online videos about those and many other things under the sun. Since 2006, WatchMojo has streamed 825 million videos, including 400 million in-stream views and 425 million in-banner impressions.[11]

And it works, to the tune of 50,000,000 global consumers per month across all platforms. No doubt part of the reason for its tremendous success is that WatchMojo videos, while focused around current and timely events, at the same time aim to provide information that's timeless and "evergreen." [12]

How They're Doing It: Video production has to be paid for. WatchMojo uses three main methods to obtain that funding: [12]

1. Licensing and syndication
2. Advertising
3. Custom promotional messages for media companies and marketers

These methods have made WatchMojo profitable since November 2010. [12]

Where They Came From: WatchMojo was founded in 2006 by entrepreneur, Ashkan Karbasfrooshan (@ashkan). According to Ashkan, the success of WatchMojo largely came from choosing to be distribution-based rather than destination-based. In other words, Watch Mojo looked around, saw YouTube—as did everyone!—and knew that merely being "us too" on the video block wouldn't be good enough. Instead of imitating the competition, Ashkan took the approach of licensing original content to other media outlets,

---

[11] http://www.prweb.com/releases/2012/5/prweb9564685.htm
[12] http://watchmojo.com/corporate/about.php

building the company's income through a cut in advertising revenue.[13]

And the result? A video enterprise that has its "Mojo" working!

[13] http://nextmontreal.com/2011/02/17/ashkan-karbasfrooshan-building-a-video-content-business-in-world-of-tech/

E-commerce

"You can't solve everyone's problems, but you need to find just enough people willing to pay you to solve theirs." ~ Unknown

Hot Clothes—On the Cheap!

Company: Jack Threads
Website: www.jackthreads.com
Last Known Revenue: Estimated between $5 and $10 Million[14]

Who They Are: JackThreads is a men's members-only, online flash-sales site with something everyone loves: BARGAINS. You say you're a hunter? JackThreads has it down to an art form. They comb the men's fashion jungle (otherwise known as the "overstock" room at top design outfits) for everything from jackets to shoes, sunglasses, and more. They do the hunting; you get the trophy—name-brand clothing at STEEP discounts of 50 to 80%.

How They're Doing It: Each day, at noon Eastern Standard Time, three to four new sales offerings go up on the site—unique assortments of apparel, sneakers, and accessories at rock-bottom retail prices. The low prices have a time limit, usually 48 to 72 hours. When that window closes, it closes—but, in the meantime, you can score some great bargains. Joining the site is free; just register. AND you get referral bonuses for bringing your friends in on the action as well!

Where They Came From: Jason Ross (@JasonPRoss), the founder of JackThreads, was an Ohio State graduate in 2003 when he started Sports Marketing Innovations with a friend. That business sold promotional products in the NCAA college market, and it worked for a time...until one morning Ross knew the passion was gone. He sold SMI, then went took some odd jobs and did some bartending to bring in cash while he mulled over a new business plan.[15]

He had seen the private shopping club business model work well in Europe, but it hadn't yet made it to the States. What if it could? What would he like to see it used for? The answer was obvious: men's fashions at reasonable prices.[14] After working on the idea for two years, he knew he was

---

[14] http://smallbusiness.aol.com/2011/02/08/jackthreads-jason-ross-how-a-kid-from-ohio-took-the-fashion-wo/
[15] http://mixergy.com/jason-ross-jackthreads-interview/

ready to launch—which the site officially did, on July 31, 2008.[14]

"Bootstrapping" can entail lots of different things. Raising capital, of course, was one part of the puzzle; one Ross managed with his earnings, profits from SMI, and a personal loan. But probably his most impressive—and creative—bootstrap moment happened when he persuaded his former OSU Computer Science professor to let the present class build the JackThreads website for him. [14]

Others have taken notice of this innovative entrepreneur: Jack Threads was acquired in 2010 by Thrillist.com, a site that e-mails recommendations and lists products and services for men in cities across the nation. Guys who are already Thrillist members, as the site says, have "found another way to be even more awesome than you already are"—and can become members of JackThreads merely be logging in with their Thrillist IDs.[14]

JackThreads' mission, as they put it, is, "We want you to look good without breaking the bank." Jason Ross found a great—and innovative—way to "bank" on that very mission...and the results look good indeed.

An Accidental Success Bringing Indie Music to the Masses

Company: CDbaby
Website: www.cdbaby.com
Last known revenue: Undisclosed

What They Do: Indie artists are all over this company! CD Baby is the leading site for selling indie music. This ingenious site allows independent-musicians a platform to promote, produce, and display their music. It allows customers to browse their database for independent music – bringing the music to the masses on one streamlined site.

How'd they do it: When Derek Sivers (@Sivers) first opened CDBaby in 1989 he was simply a musical artist who was trying to get his music out there to be purchased without having to deal with the hectic world of music producing. He wanted a way to do this without selling out to the big labels and he was sick of not being able to contact other artists or sell his music to whomever he wanted. At the time, there just wasn't an available outlet that was comparable for him. When he arrived on the scene, a new artist had very little chance of getting 'made' in the business.

Sivers' brainchild was CDbaby which eventually gartered interest from other independent musicians seeking to produce their music in a similar fashion. Over time the collection of artists grew as did the fans. CDbaby now has a massive pool of indie artists and is known for their excellent customer service. Their representatives actually listen to the music listed and customers can ask for advice on a music selection and they can be directed. Customers and musicians alike rave about the site because it's easy to use and completely unfettered by the prices and influence of the mainstream music scene.

After the hype about the site got big enough, CDbaby was sold off. Bidding wars began and in the end Sivers was able to sell CDbaby for $22 million![16] Most of the money that he received was placed into a trust that was set aside for charity. But the feats which he accomplished to make this happen are no less than amazing. He

---

[16] http://www.venturevoice.com/2008/10/vv_show_50_derek_sivers_of_cd.html

decided to write a book about his experiences in which he tells the tale of how it all began. In the book he gave several suggestions for new artists and entrepreneurs to help them out.

His advice started with – try out your hypothesis. If you have a plan, try it out, test it on others, and see how it might work.[17]

Next: Move forward with the plan only if you have a significant following who are willing to pay for the effort that you are going to need to make.[17]

And finally... Consider creating an actual practice run of your work, a prototype or an example and then get it out there as fast as you can. In this business, advertising is like starting a fire, if you can catch a spark, you have to keep feeding it to get it to grow. [17]

---

[17] http://personalexcellence.co/blog/interview-cd-baby/

Pulling a T-Shirt Company Up by Its "Bootstraps"

Company name: Custom Ink
Website: www.customink.com
Last Known Revenue: $61.7 Million (2009)[18]

Who Are They? CustomInk, a custom T-shirt e-commerce company, is the place where groups, teams, businesses, and anyone else with a "message" can come to create awesome personalized T-shirts — over 15 *million* of 'em, as a matter of fact, since their founding in 2001.[19] Named Washington, D.C.'s "hottest bootstrap" in 2010, CustomInk is ranked as one of the largest 200 e-commerce companies in the world by *Internet Retailer*.[20]

How They've Done It: The CustomInk story began in 1999, with three former college classmates who'd just graduated from Harvard the year before. Eventual co-founder and president Marc Katz (@marc_katz) was wheeling and dealing on Wall Street but itched to be an entrepreneur, to have an occupation with "heart" and meaning. Meanwhile (unbeknownst to Marc), his former roommate, Mike Driscoll , built the initial version of CustomInk.com over the summer, had a handful of customers, and wanted a way to grow it.[21]

The problem? Mike had one foot out the door on the way back to grad school, but when he talked to Marc about their success to date and making a "real business" out of it...something clicked. Helping people create an item that was original, personal, and wearable made sense to Marc. This, he could get excited about. Wasting no time, he got in touch with a third Harvard alum, Dave Christensen, and invited him on board. Soon (in late 2000, to be exact) CustomInk's first fully functional site launched, and the adventure began.[21]

Did we say "adventure"? It was that and more. Lacking any sophisticated business systems at the beginning, the

---

[18] http://www.inc.com/inc5000/profile/customink
[19] http://www.crunchbase.com/company/customink
[20] http://www.internetretailer.com/top500/list/
[21] http://mixergy.com/marc-katz-customink-interview/

fledgling team of 10 (including Marc and Dave) entered orders and manually calculated due dates and shipping times — on paper. Phones were yet another challenge: when a customer called the 800 number, the phone rang simultaneously *on the desk of everyone in the company.* Adventure? Yep. They had it. [21]

Auspicious, it may not have been. Flashy, it definitely wasn't. But from the start, CustomInk's staff worked hard to do a great job for their customers — and it's a focus they keep to this day.

Father and Son Duo Bootstrap to Success

Company: PremiumBeat
Website: www.premiumbeat.com
Last Known Revenue: $1 Million (2011)[22]

What They Do: PremiumBeat sells royalty-free music online. With revenues of around $1 Million and profits at near $350,000, PremiumBeat has proven that selling online digital music is a very profitable and scalable business model.[22]

How They're Doing It: Created in 2005 by father and son duo Gilles Arbour (father) and Francois Arbour (@francoisarbour), PremiumuBeat was born when Francois got the idea while searching for music to use in advertising videos that he was working on at the time. Because of the challenge he had in *finding* royalty-free music that he could use, he knew there was a problem in the market. Where there is a problem, there is an opportunity to provide a much-desired solution. [22]

In Francois' own words, "I was really having a hard time finding good music and also the big problem was you had to click through a thousand tracks before you found the one you needed. I knew a couple of composers and I decided to contact them and said, 'Hey, would you want to sell your music online?' Since I had a good relationship with this particular artist, he said yes. So I talked to my father. I pitched him the idea, and he was like, 'Yeah...'" [22]

It took Francois and Gilles a mind-numbing 5,000 - 10,000 hours to build their first version of the website, which launched with only 45 music tracks. Their first customers came through Google Adwords. They realized early on that banner advertising simply didn't work. What they were spending on them would only yield a handful of new customers. So the founders focused their efforts back on the advertising they knew worked - Adwords and focused on optimizing their customer conversion by running a lot of

---

[22] http://mixergy.com/francois-arbour-premiumbeat-interview/

A/B testing on their landing pages until they found a recipe for success.[22]

Francois is quoted as saying: "One huge thing is when you do something just yourself and you don't owe anything to anyone, it's pretty hard to push yourself to put it on. I had people pushing me, so I just put it online. At some point, we were like, 'All right, let's put it online. Let's get it started and see how high it goes.'" [22]

They found yet another need out there, and set their sights on fulfilling that need…full-on!

The Custom Dress Shirt House that "Gets" You!

Company: Blank Label
Website: www.blanklabel.com
Last Known Revenue: ~$1 Million (2011 projection) [23]

Who They Are: Blank Label is a group of folks who want to make your next custom dress shirt. Why? Because, as they put it, they *get* you—as opposed to "expensive, large, disconnected brands who don't get you anymore because they're spending too much time on their boats." [24] Don't get them wrong...they'd love to be on a boat. But when and if they do, they'll "invite you to the party, because we're in this together." [24]

How They're Doing It: They make it possible—nay, *easy!*—for you to select your fabric, buttons, collar types, and stitching to design your own shirt on their website. Shirts are stitched in Shanghai and shipped directly to customers for a fraction of the price charged for custom dress shirts at traditional retailers.

Although the shirts are not cheap—they range from $60 to $145, depending on the fabric—lots of little "extras" are included. Monogramming or other customizations are free, as is standard shipping. And, because custom clothing design can be a tricky thing, should something go wrong, they'll remake the shirt for you—and send the old one to a charity. In that case, both domestic and international return shipping is free to the customer.

They're doing it right: in 2010, the company generated $450,000 in sales and was projected to more than double to $1 Million by the end of 2011.[23] And they're not finished, either: the company also plans to launch custom women's blouses soon.

Where They Came From: Blank Label founder Fan Bi (@lifeofbi) was a student at Babson College when, at the ripe old age of 23, he already knew that the best-looking dress shirts were custom-made. But they were over-the-top pricey as well! Thus began the nagging question, "How can I make the luxury of custom affordable?" It nagged at him so thoroughly that Bi skipped his last year at Babson,

[23] http://images.businessweek.com/slideshows/20110915/2011-finalists-america-s-best-young-entrepreneurs#slide6
[24] http://www.crunchbase.com/company/blank-label

took $35,000 that he'd saved from working in high school and college, and launched the Label that Would Be Blank in 2009.[23]

The company generated over $125K in revenue in their first six months—without a scrap of advertising. Even today, they say they've still not "spent any real money" on advertising.[25]

---

[25] http://mixergy.com/blank-label-danny-wong-interview/

Tools and Education for "Wanta-preneurs"

Company: AppSumo
Website: www.appsumo.com
Last Known Revenue: >$1 Million[26]

Who They Are: AppSumo is the place for wantra-preneurs and small business people to come for discounts (all the way down to F-R-E-E) on bright, bouncing bundles of software — AND instruction on growing your business, from I-*Think-I-Can* to *Hot Dang! I Did It!*

How They Do It: So it's a deal site. Big whoop. Are you yawning yet? Well, don't nod off before you hear about how AppSumo is different from the gazillion other "deal" sites out there.

It's a matter of two things. First, their focus: selling and promoting digital goods. Second, their time frames: the deals aren't limited to "today only" or until the requisite quota of participants "click through." With AppSumo, you've got time to consider the deal— much more time than with your garden-variety "deal" site.

In return for these good deals and this extra breathing room, AppSumo makes its money through commissions generated on the sales it makes for its business partners.

Where They Came From: AppSumo was the brainchild of Noah Kagan (@noahkagan) and David Cramer in March 2010.[26]

Kagan, an early Facebook and Mint.com employee, started AppSumo after realizing that of all the deal sites out there, NONE dealt with the growing Web app and software categories. The original core vision was to help solve distribution dilemmas for startups — and eventually all digital goods — by providing discounts on their products to AppSumo's audience.

Meanwhile, after some conversation with Mark Zuckerberg of Facebook, Kagan tweaked the vision to focus solely on growth, specifically of AppSumo's email list.[27] To accomplish this, Kagan juiced up the advertising budget, largely through "free deals" that achieved high conversion rates and led to more long-term

---

[26] http://en.wikipedia.org/wiki/AppSumo
[27] http://www.founderly.com/2011/08/noah-kagan-appsumo-2-of-2/

customers.[28] In addition, he increased how often AppSumo got out both advertising and customer email reminders.

Speaking of email — that's the key to AppSumo's success. In its first year, Kagan and Cramer were able to acquire 200,000 email addresses of interested consumers to whom they wanted to market their software and education courses. At first, AppSumo focused only on digital tools, such as apps. Soon, however — in an "aha" moment, as described by Kagan —the company found that their largest response came from their learning offerings.[27] These include everything an entrepreneur needs to get a flying start: from copywriting to validating business ideas — with the bonus of AppSumo and Mint.com sharing the story of THEIR growth through smart marketing.

 In short, whether it's software or a supportive bit of information you need to get your startup off the ground...AppSumo might well be the "gold mine" resource to put you over the top!

---

[28] http://www.marketingshow.com/internet-entrepreneur-noah-kagan-on-business-failure-marketing-plan/

"Springing" from Failure to $45 Million

Company: Fast Spring
Website: www.fastspring.com
Last Known Revenue: >$45 Million[29]

Who They Are: FastSpring is CEO Dan Engel (@fastspringceo) and a host of other people who offer an innovative e-commerce engine that's designed to optimize ease of use and customer service while cutting costs as well. For vendors of downloadable products such as software, games, and e-books, they're a boon; for companies who need customized order pages, they are a valued partner. And they're the #1 e-commerce service for Mac software publishers.[30]

How They're Doing It: By happy customer word-of-mouth, among other things. Over 10,000 clients have signed up for FastSpring since 2005, and the company has been profitable since 2009. This prosperity doesn't happen by accident, but by focus: the four founders are actually located in four entirely different states, and their 25 staff members are scattered as well. Many staff members work from home, and no "office" of the company has more than two or three people in it![29]

Nevertheless, that focus works. FastSpring was ranked 53 in *Inc. Magazine*'s Inc. 500 list of fastest-growing companies in the US for 2011[31] and the #1 fastest-growing company on California's Central Coast by the *Pacific Coast Business Times*. In 2010, they were listed #41 and #2 in these rankings, respectively. In addition, Deloitte ranked FastSpring the #1 fastest-growing company in the Greater Los Angeles area and #13 in North America (U.S. and Canada), in its 2011 Technology Fast 500™ awards.

Where They Came From: FastSpring began in 2005 through the efforts of current CEO Dan Engel and 3 others who had a cumulative experience of over 40 years in the e-commerce industry. Dan's startups hadn't been entirely successful before this. He started an online magazine subscription business, GrapeApe.com, with his brother while in college. The good news? It nearly sold to Amazon for millions. The bad news? It ended up folding after running out of money.

[29] http://mixergy.com/dan-engel-fastspring-interview/
[30] http://www.fastspring.com/company.php
[31] http://www.inc.com/inc5000/profile/fastspring

After swallowing his pride, Dan picked his head up and went to work for an employer to bring in some needed income at the time. In the meantime, he networked and pitched the idea for FastSpring to some other entrepreneurial types.

In the meantime, Dan was living off payouts from working for two companies—GoToMyPC and Picasa[31]—that also were acquired by larger firms. The bottom line? All four founders put in $10,000 each and FastSpring "sprang" into being. If bootstrapping is the epitome of optimism and opportunity, Dan Engel's success is a prime example of both optimism and a truism: "If at first you don't succeed..."[29]

That optimism has clearly paid off, in more ways than one.

"Sparking" Software Success

Company: SparkFun Electronics
Website: www.SparkFun.com
Last Known Revenue: $18 Million (2010)[32]

Who They Are: SparkFun is a group of companies that makes electronic component modules and devices all over the world. SparkFun helps customers assemble all kinds of projects, from an earthquake data logger to a high-altitude balloon to a touchscreen mouse. Products include things like resistors, LEDs, humidity sensors, and LCD screens which are sold to crafters, designers, artists, DJs, teachers, professors, and engineers. In addition to online tutorials, SparkFun now offers classes, too—an all-around approach that has brought in revenues approaching $18 million in 2010.[33]

Where They Came From: Nathan Seidle (@chipaddict) founded SparkFun in 2003, while still a student at the University of Colorado. As with many entrepreneurs, he decided to solve a problem that particularly frustrated him: the current state of the Internet's e-commerce solutions for electronic replacement parts. When there's a problem, there's a better way to do it, **Error! Bookmark not defined.** so Seidle set out to find that "better way." [33]

SparkFun started small, with about $2,500 in credit card debt as financing. "I believe about $2000 went to inventory purchases" Seidle explains, "and $500 went to infrastructure including $25 for a scale, $15 for a tape gun, etc. I forgot to buy boxes to actually ship product to customers. How I made it this far is good fodder for pundits." [33]

After the inventory sold, it was a matter of repeating the process. "You take all the money you make and buy more inventory with it," Seidle goes on. "You continue to do this until either you have enough inventory to cover the number of incoming orders, or you want to eat. I think it was more than 3 years before I was able to buy a new winter jacket. A growing, bootstrapped business is a cash-devouring machine." [33]

---

[32] http://tumblr.iamdanw.com/post/9262050709/SparkFun-electronics-inc-founded-in-2003-in
[33] http://37signals.com/svn/posts/2896-bootstrapped-profitable-proud-SparkFun-/

Siedle's advice for you? [33]

Focus. "Do one thing well. You may be good at many things, but the free market is a harsh place for amateurs. Find the thing you are best at and drive that product, service, or talent home. We are best at designing our own products and producing our own products. When SparkFun began, we tried doing consulting work and wasted a lot of time and energy. As soon as you establish something is not your core, quickly leave it behind.

FISI = *fuck it ship it*. I stole this term from a friend of mine named CTP. He was referring to engineers' constant want to revise something. How often do we find ourselves saying: 'Give me two more days and I can add so much functionality!' Whether you are a programmer, graphic designer, or chef, at some point you have to ship the thing. Remember FISI, or else you will very quickly hit the bankruptcy wall."

Seek help. "I ignored this in the beginning, but ultimately I searched out business groups and other business owners that I could talk to. Once your business starts to groove, you'll discover all sorts of problems you never knew where coming. Wild success can feel paradoxically lonely at the onset. Fellow peers in the business world can help a lot for moral support and problem solving."

"Letter Hunting" to a $10 Million Success Story!

Company: Sticks and Stones
Website: www.createsticksandstones.com
Last known revenue: $10.5 Million (2010)[34]

Who They Are: Sticks and Stones is a family-owned business of folks who create art from letter photography. In the process of "letter hunting"™, they find letter forms in nature (STICKS) and architecture (STONES), photograph them, and make them into unique, distinctive pieces for "people who have everything."

How They're Doing It: Jera Deal (@sticksstones) and her husband, Brad, started their company in 2005, when Jera began letter-hunting with her children at parks and various places to teach them the alphabet. Brad, the girls, and his wife continue to letter hunt™, as new alphabet photography is constantly being added to the "Letters Gallery."

Where They Came From: When Jera took her oldest daughter "letter hunting," it was merely a way for the 15-month-old to learn the alphabet by finding letters in nature and with architecture. As a classroom mom, Jera was responsible for purchasing a gift for a teacher who was getting married. Jera made a beautiful frame and gathered some of the pictures her daughters and she had taken to form the teacher's new last name. From that one creation, they received multiple orders and knew immediately they had something special.[35]

But just how special? They were soon to find out—through a showbiz connection.

Following the 2005 launch of their website, they got into their first catalog and set out to get their product into as many hands as possible. There was one person, however, who they especially wanted to reach: Oprah Winfrey. After a few trips to her show and "a little bit of luck and persistence," says Brad, they finally managed to have contact with the media icon herself. [34]

---

[34] http://www.entrepreneur.com/article/196304
[35] http://www.marthastewart.com/269162/sticks-and-stones-alphabet-letter-signs

"I stood up in front of 300 audience members and [gave] her a keepsake," Brad explains. "She opened it and loved it"—so much so that she commissioned one on the spot for Tom Cruise and Katie Holmes. "We were already self-sustaining at that point, but having [Oprah's approval] helped tremendously."[34]

Amazon.Com for Artists: One Man, $200, and a Dream

Company: Fine Art America
Website: www.fineartamerica.com
Last Known Revenue: $2.5M (2010)[37]

Who Are They: FineArtAmerica.com is what happens when one man dreams: now, it has changed the way artwork is bought and sold around the world.

What They Do: FineArtAmerica.com makes art commerce as simple as a few mouse clicks: artists and photographers upload their images to FineArtAmerica.com, set their price, and in a matter of seconds, they're selling to collectors anywhere across the globe— with no hassle. Fine Art America does the grunt work: printing, framing, matting, packaging, shipping, and payment collections. From their North Carolina production facility, they print and send the art out "ready-to-hang" — with a 30-day money-back guarantee.

And...There's More! Besides providing an online marketplace and fulfillment service, Fine Art America also "feeds" artists and photographers valuable sales and marketing tools to streamline and speed up their careers — info like how to set up branded Web stores, sell prints on Facebook and Amazon, and create e-newsletters.[36]

...Much More! At present, more than 85,000 artists and photographers offer two million images for sale on FineArtAmerica.com. Visitors stop in not only to purchase prints from this ever-expanding collection but for a little "schmoozing" as well — socializing and networking with both fellow artists and other collectors. [37]

Where They Came From: Fine Art America is the brainchild of Sean Broihier, who saw the Big Apple as the land of opportunity, landed there fresh out of college with a couple hundred bucks to his name, took a job as an engineer, and

---

[36] http://www.businesswire.com/news/home/20111215005948/en/Fine-Art-America-Signs-Licensing-Agreement-National

spent nights and weekends teaching himself to program websites. Then, in 2007, the idea for Fine Art America took hold of him — after he put together a website for his brother, who worked for a Chicago art gallery — and wouldn't let go. He built a platform for people to upload text and images to the Web...and the rest is history.[37]

Lucrative history, at that. Profitable from day one, Fine Art America went from revenues of $175,000 in 2008 to $1 million in 2009, and projected a cool $2.5 million for 2010.[37]

[37] http://fineartamerica.com/showmessages.php?messageid=271354

Reducing the "Don't Like" List...One Wine at a Time

Company: Garagiste
Website: www.garagiste.com
Last Known Revenue: $30 Million (2012)[38]

Who They Are: Jon Rimmerman (@Garagiste_Wine) is the driving sommelier behind Garagiste, a company that sends out daily e-mails about great deals on great wines. Having developed his palate in a college wine-tasting club, Rimmerman decided to continue sharing wine info via a faxed letter to friends. Hence was born a "daily deal" source, before the term "daily deal site" was part of our vernacular.

How They're Doing It: Garagiste has taken a very "club like" approach to its clientele and flown below the radar on purpose. While the company has been around since 2006, it wasn't until 2010 that they developed a website. Prior to that, their e-mail list was so exclusive that the only way to get on it was to be referred by a current subscriber! Today, the newsletter has over 100,000 subscribers who happily "drink up" Garagiste's exclusive deals on small-production wines from around the world.[38]

It's "dirty, thankless" work Rimmerman does: traveling the globe, tasting new wines and making new connections in the industry. All of this hard time is done in the name of introducing his customers to new and enticing wines not sold in the grocery store. With the middlemen (and women) gone from the equation, Rimmerman then offers lower prices at higher profit margins—becoming the "Sub Pop Records of the wine trade," scouting talent, and connecting old-school vintners to discriminating consumers. [38]

Where They Came From: From law school, of course—doesn't your sommelier have a J.D.? Actually, all kidding aside, Rimmerman went from law school to working at Starbucks. There, in the figurative shadow of Howard Schultz, Jon didn't take long to realize that the wine letter he'd started was a great first step in getting his "startup" started up! He'd already made the jump from faxes to e-mail, and that newsletter had grown through word-of-mouth; it wasn't a big leap to imagine leveraging the e-mail list to becoming an actual wine seller. Rimmerman claims that he made two lists — things he

---

[38] http://www.nytimes.com/2012/10/14/magazine/jon-rimmerman-garagiste.html?pagewanted=all&_r=0

liked about the wine business and things he did not — and decided that his company's goal would be to transform the industry until his "don't like" column was empty. [38]

The story so far? Garagiste is on lots and LOTS of wine-lovers' "like" lists already, and more every day. We'll drink to that!

Consumer Internet

"If we did all the things we are capable of doing, we would literally astound ourselves." ~Thomas Edison

An Email That Gives You Discounts To Premium Restaurants

Company: Blackboard Eats
Website: www.blackboardeats.com
Last Known Revenue: Undisclosed

What They Do: Blackboard Eats is a free e-mail subscription service that delivers exclusive deals at top restaurants, and reviews on the best artisanal culinary products – currently in 4 cities (New York, San Francisco, Chicago, and L.A.).

Blackboard Eats features deals at high-end restaurants that don't normally offer coupons and discounts. Subscribers receive a weekly e-mail detailing a local restaurant promotion, and they have a limited amount of time to request a free passcode for the deal. To redeem the promotion, they give the passcode to the restaurant when they make a reservation, or arrive for their meal. [39]

Revenues are earned from email advertising and "sponsored specials" at restaurants. The company also earns around 25-30% of the revenues from their sponsored specials, which are featured at 8 restaurants per month in each city. [39]

For the *exclusive* deals that get highlighted on Blackboard Eats' weekly or twice-weekly e-mails, restaurants get to keep *all* of the revenue they receive from the promotions. The deals can range from 30 percent off, to a special dish. [39]

How They Do It: Founded by Maggie Nemser (@maggienemser) in 2009, Blackboard Eats has amassed a cult-like following in the 5 cities it currently covers. It currently has well over 50,000 email subscribers! Maggie was a former food editor at Yahoo!, where she received a ton of emails from local PR reps representing these great restaurants. After doing some initial research, she realized there was no one-stop shop of highly curated, exclusive specials to high end restaurants in the city. Knock! Knock! Opportunity calling! [39]

---

[39] http://articles.chicagotribune.com/2011-07-21/news/chi-blackboardeats-deal-site-arrives-in-chicago-starting-with-ing-20110720_1_blackboardeats-gilt-city-groupon

Maggie staffed Blackboard Eats with some of the best food editors around – with writers from publications like Gourmet, Daily Candy, Zagat, and Food and Wine. [40]

[40] http://econsultancy.com/us/blog/5831-q-a-black-board-eats-ceo-maggie-nemser

Making Reading Easy Again

Company: BookSwim
Website: www.bookswim.com
Last Known Revenue: Undisclosed

Who They Are: BookSwim is a group of folks who saw a successful "rental" model in Netflix and an opportunity to apply it to books. You select books you'd like to get, and BookSwim sends you those books. You return them when you are done, and you receive your next shipment. And so on, and so on, and...

How They're Doing It: Pricing plans start at $23.95/month for up to 3 books at a time, or you can opt in for the $59.95/month plan for up to 11 books at a time. BookSwim's primary audience is upper-middle-class women (80% of subscribers are female) who belong to book clubs and are in the market for new and best-selling mass-market book titles.[41]

While its primary focus is the rental-and-return business, the company does offer a purchase option to subscribers as well. So if you truly *can't* bear to part with that book, you can simply add it to your monthly bill—a doubly convenient option.

Where They Came From: George Burke (@geoburke) and Shamoon Siddiqui, two college friends, got the BookSwim idea in 2006 while "freeloading" at bookstores, drinking the coffee and reading. When asked if they were paying for the books with their coffee, they said, "Nope. We're just reading them here."

Now this kind of behavior should never be condoned. But George and Shamoon noticed a pattern: everyone else was doing it, even if they didn't admit it so frankly. There were reasons: the local libraries closed their doors long before most people got home from work—or, if they were open, they had waiting lists months long for the latest bestsellers. On the other hand, bookstores charged too much for the books for most people to buy all they wanted to read. George and Shamoon decided there had to be a better way.

---

[41] SubscriptionSiteInsider.com Case Study

So, using $6,500 of their own money (they've never taken any outside financing), they took the plunge. In March 2007, BookSwim mailed out its first rental book, *The Richest Man in Babylon*. That began an odyssey of "crates of books in the basement" that has taken off like a shot, as tens of thousands of readers have discovered the affordability and convenience of at-home book rental.[42]

Prior to launching the site, Burke was a Web developer and Internet marketer with a specialty in search engine optimization. He credits the company's chairman, former publishing executive Georg Richter, for helping him learn the intricacies of the book publishing world and the online subscription industry— for example, understanding the importance of credit card processing when running a recurring-billing service. "You learn by doing, and when it's your own money on the line, you pay attention to it very much."[41]

Recently, Shamoon sold his interest in BookSwim to Burke, but the two remain close...and now they can afford to buy books in droves!

---

[42] http://www.bookswim.com/about.html

Finding the "Gold" in Lead Management

Company: Insurance Agents
Website: www.insuranceagents.com
Last Known Revenue: $11.8 million (2009)[43]

Who They Are: InsuranceAgents.com is a site founded in 2003 that allows consumers to compare insurance quotes from multiple insurance agents. More specifically, it's Seth Kravitz (@SecondCityCEO) and Lev Barinskiy (@lbarinskiy)—and a whole lot of other nice folks who've brought InsuranceAgents.com to the *Inc.* 500 list as one of the fastest-growing privately-held companies in the U.S.[43]

How They're Doing It: From a website that features agent-friendly customer service and payment plans—and leads that are worth their weight in gold. One insurance agent, Sam Goldsmith, who runs an insurance agency in Indianapolis, spends $3,000 a month on leads from Barinskiy and Kravitz's website and is happy to do it. "I rely on their business to produce leads and feed my family," he says, "and I run my business off of their marketing." [43]

Where They Came From: Lev was an Allstate insurance agent in Ohio when he realized that there was money to be made managing leads for agents—more money than he could make managing his own insurance business. He bankrolled his initial venture with earnings from his AllState business, combined with other projects that still took a lot of attention. Kravitz, meanwhile, worked on websites designed to drive insurance shoppers to lead-generation sites. There, a shopper entered personal data which was then sold to agents prospecting in that shopper's area.[44]

But by 2007, Barinskiy and Kravitz saw that the potential profits were higher selling customer information directly to agents, rather than acting as a middleman. At that point, Lev handed off his insurance agency to his brother and made the startup his top priority. That new business model spawned the new site, InsuranceLeadz.com, in 2007.[44]

---

[43] http://www.inc.com/inc5000/profile/insuranceagentscom
[44] http://37signals.com/svn/posts/2691-bootstrapped-profitable-proud-insuranceagentscom

Over the next 12 months or so, annual revenue rocketed from $700,000 to nearly $12 million, and payroll expanded from six to 35 employees. The number of leads sold each month tripled, to 150,000, and the website was adding 300 new agents per month. "We definitely felt a little invincible because of how fast the company was growing," Kravitz says. [44]

InsuranceAgents.com has good reason to feel a touch "bulletproof" at this point: with the Inc. 500 recognition, this business's growth shows no signs of slowing down—and insurance businesses all over the country are growing as well because of it. Talk about win-win!

Barinskiy and Kravitz made out pretty selling their then 8-year old baby Insurance Agents to Bankrate.com for an undisclosed sum.

Rescue Me!

Company: GiftCardRescue
Website: www.giftcardrescue.com
Last Known Revenue: $550,000 (2009)[45]

Who They Are: Quite simply, GiftCardRescue is a company that's all about options! Imagine this scenario: Aunt Sophie buys you a gift card from "Kitchen Stuff R Us," only your idea of "cooking" is setting out two #10 "Meal Deals" on plastic-coated paper plates. What to do? This is where GiftCardRescue comes in. They'll take that culinary equipment card off your hands, at a slight discount from its face value, and give you the cash. Then, the bride-to-be down the street who is craving one of those super-duper top-of-the-line blenders goes to GiftCardRescue, purchases your card, and shops happily off into the sunset. Everyone wins: you don't feel guilty—you can tell Aunt Sophie that you "got exactly what you wanted" out of the card; the bride gets her shiny new blender; and GiftCardRescue profits from the small spread between the purchase price they gave you and their reselling price.

How They're Doing It: Giving the people what they want! You can get up to 90% cash back for your unwanted gift cards *and* save from 4% up to 30% on discounted gift cards to over 350 national merchants who earn a percentage of revenue from each transaction.

Where They Came From: The mind of Kwame Kuadey (@KwameKuadey), actually. No stranger to the business world, Kwame graduated from the John Hopkins MBA program, then worked at Citigroup as a compliance manager, but quickly found the entrepreneurial "itch" too strong to ignore. 46

The idea for GiftCardRescue took shape in 2008, after he listened to friends moan about having gift cards they really didn't want but couldn't use anywhere but at the retailers involved, he started thinking about changing that. Kwame

---

[45] http://www.forbes.com/byb/2009/semi/boost-your-business-contest-09-giftcardrescue.html
[46] http://www.bmoremedia.com/features/giftcardrescue052411.aspx

took $95,000 of his own money—cobbled together from credit cards, generous family, and friends—and jumped in[45] with no outside capital at all.[47] But it was clearly an idea whose time had come: in the company's first year, even with very little advertising, they sold $55,000 in gift cards and were on track to sell $100,000 in 2009. They expected to break even in 2009 with a projected 13% profit on $550,000 in revenue. In 2009-10, revenue increased 400%.[46]

Kwame leveraged his quick wits as a bootstrapping entrepreneur to shave costs by shooting his own video content and creating the largest blog devoted to gift cards. While it wasn't easy to manage all of this on his own, the efforts paid off. [46]

In Their Own Words:
"What I realized is that there are a lot of misconceptions out there on how startups are portrayed," Kuadey says. "There is this hysteria that all you need is a good idea, and then you can write a business plan and get funding. The reality is that 90% of business startups are bootstrapped by money from friends and family. It's going to be a grind." [46]

GiftCardRescue may have been a "grind" to start…but it's "gifting" a lot of people from its success!

[47] http://www.giftcardrescue.com/about

A Classroom Idea That Brought in Millions

Company: GiftZip.com
Website: www.giftzip.com
Last Known Revenue: Undisclosed

Who They Are: GiftZip is an online portal to instant gift cards from hundreds of retailers. They do not sell gift cards themselves, but instead redirect visitors to the merchant's website for checkout. An instant gift card is purchased online and can be emailed or printed—and it's all free of charge, with no registration required.

How They're Doing It: GiftZip earns a commission from the retailer every time they direct a customer to their website who ends up purchasing an online gift card.

"We did an extensive search as to which retailers offer an instant gift card,"[48] says founder Sam Hogg. "The site is just a portal. We are currently driving traffic to retailers' sites free of charge. Our commitment is to make the site always free to the user." The simplicity made GiftZip a 2008 holiday hit, netting over 10,000 visitors in the three weeks leading up to Christmas. [48]

And word has gotten around to the merchants: since its founding, GiftZip's use has increased 2,100 percent, and it's grown from 120 to 275 retailers.[49]

Where They Came From: Sam Hogg conceived of the idea of GiftZip in 2008, sitting in a sustainable supply chain class during business school at Michigan State.[48] Opening his wallet, he stared at one of several plastic gift cards he had received for Christmas, thinking how wasteful the cards were. And he was right: according to the International Card Manufacturing Association, almost 17 billion plastic cards, including gift, library, video rental, and membership cards, were produced in 2006 alone.

What if there was a better way to handle gift-giving than all this individual plastic?

---

[48]
http://www.mlive.com/environment/index.ssf/2009/02/sam_hogg_and_giftzipcom_becaus.html

That started the wheels turning in his head—and, instead of paying attention in class, Hogg began forming a business model. His decided to curate and build an online database of online gift cards from major retail outlets. His website placed competing retailers next to one another, a model recommended by a college marketing professor, who suggested consumers are more likely to buy a product when given multiple choices, even if those choices sit next to competing brands. And, despite daydreaming through at least one class, he even got ongoing support from the professors and classmates at his alma mater. "You don't need an MBA to start a business," he says, "but I couldn't have gotten that from scratching my head in a basement."[49]

Sam sold GiftZip to gift card giant SVM in 2011, just two years after startup, for an undisclosed—but presumably healthy—sum. He admits that when faced with the prospect of selling his baby, at first he considered raising venture capital to continue to expand it. In the end, however, he believed that selling would provide him with the best return possible. [50] Sounds like his "gift" for innovation has proven him right!

---

[49] http://www.entrepreneur.com/article/207004#
[50] http://www.msnbc.msn.com/id/44753247/ns/business-small_business/t/why-i-decided-take-money-sell-my-startup/#.UOpKY3fAEaU

The Sweet Sound of Turning a $70 Investment into Millions

Company: Hear and Play
Website: www.hearandplay.com
Last Known Revenue: ~$3.5 Million (2012)[51]

Who They Are: Hear and Play is a musical place: it has a captive customer base of enthusiastic musicians around the world who are learning to play the piano not by sight, but "by ear."

How They're Doing It: Hear and Play says that "If you can hear it, you can play it." Their modus operandi is enabling ordinary people to learn to play anything by ear—without having to use sheet music!—through their lesson programs that range from $19 to $40 a month. They also offer blogs, articles, and other resources, including performance tips, for a wide variety of music from jazz, rock, hip hop, and salsa to gospel and blues. And it's working: more than 2 million aspiring musicians download the online lessons every year, and over 300,000 loyal students receive their regular newsletters. [51]

Where They Came From: Founder Jermaine Griggs (@realhearandplay), a pianist and musician, began his business twelve years ago with $70 he earned from playing music at a local church. Investing that money in buying the website domain hearandplay.com was the easy part! Next, to actually use the URL, the 16-year-old fledgling businessman had to learn HTML.[51]

"I didn't know anything [about it]," he admits, "but, you know, I figured out how to do three tables, so it was like this three- table site and it had these black bars all over the place." [51] If that doesn't sound visually appealing...it wasn't! The first iteration of the website was "quite ugly," but it was the home base he needed to start selling music online. [51]

Once the site was up and running, it was time to attract customers. Griggs used Internet "guerilla marketing" tactics to get the word out: participating in online forums, posting messages and spreading his name. He sent an initial email to 700 subscribers in his Yahoo music group—and the next day had $1,100 in sales. That start

---

[51] http://mixergy.com/jermaine-griggs-hearandplay-interview/

helped give Griggs the confidence to continue to grow and scale the business. He continued to drive traffic to the website through SEO tactics, PPC advertising, and an online affiliate program. [51]

His initial product did so well (nearly $200,000 in sales) that he decided to create and launch a second product for his current customers. By collecting email addresses from his first offering, Griggs was able to quickly realize sales on the second "go -'round" from customers already interested in what he was selling. [51]

However, like many businesses, Hear and Play suffered a sales drop-off during the recession in 2008. At that point, Griggs realized he needed to shift his business model from one-time sales to recurring revenue. That new model has enabled Hear and Play not only to survive but to thrive despite any persistent slowness in the economy; today, Hear and Play has an array of over 20 products for sale through the website.

What does Griggs say to other prospective entrepreneurs? His short and sweet advice is, "Don't wait."
"It's never going to be the right time," he says. It's never going to be— everything's never going to be perfect, so you just got to do it, get started. That is better than perfect." [51]

Starting with a dream of getting to "the other (better) side of the tracks," Jermaine Griggs now brings music into people's lives every single day. Not a bad way to make lots and *lots* of people's dreams come true!

"Blazingly Easy" Computer Backup!

Company: BackBlaze
Website: www.backblaze.com
Last Known Revenue: Undisclosed

Who They Are: Co-founded in 2007 by Gleb Budman (@GlebBudman), Brian Wilson, Tim Nufire (@TNufire), and Casey Jones, BackBlaze is a group of savvy folks who claim to have put together the ultimate "lazy" user's way to back up digital files and documents: it's automatic! Think of BackBlaze as a "bank vault" for all the valuable "stuff" on your computer.

How They're Doing It: At a lower price than any of their competitors—as low as $3.96 per month. No, they didn't pick this figure out of the air; they arrived at it by surveying potential users for the "breaking point" at which people became less likely to sign up for online backup. That "breaking point," as it turns out, is $5 per month. Staying within that neighborhood, people will actually USE the backup service...rather than just talk about it. [52]

And the "blaze" has spread like the proverbial wildfire: BackBlaze experienced a 100% growth in 2011.[53] One reason for such a growth rate, of course, is that the system is easy! Another aid to quick growth is an affiliate partner program. For each referral an affiliate provides BackBlaze, they earn a percentage of that referred customer's payments each month...for LIFE.

Now THERE's backup that pays off!

Where They Came From: Where else? From seeing one of their friends tortured by having lost data. This prompted the obvious question to friends and colleagues, "So what are you doing to prevent this happening to you?" Amazingly enough, what they heard most often was, "Nothing."

---

[52] http://www.wired.com/cloudline/2011/10/backblazes-basic-cloud/
[53] http://blog.backblaze.com/category/startup-life/

This wasn't because people didn't know online backup existed, either. In essence, that answer told the BackBlaze crew that people wanted backup systems they didn't have to THINK about.[53] So that's what the guys gave them, from the ground up...literally. The team had to custom-build their system, since the options already in place—such as Amazon—cost too much for them to use and still stay below their customers' "breaking point."

Did they have reason to think they could pull this off? You betcha: They'd previously worked together to found MailFrontier, which was acquired by SonicWall.[54] As they put it: "We wanted to build a successful, profitable company that customers loved—and did not want to risk being forced to 'exit.' Thus, we chose up front not to raise VC (venture capital) funding. We wanted to be able to take the company public, be acquired, or run it forever—whatever ended up being best for the team, our customers, and our partners."[54]

Looks like it's catching fire!

---

[54] http://www.backblaze.com/team.html

It's a Vintage Day in the Neighborhood

Company: Local Wine Events
Website: www.localwineevents.com
Last Known Revenue: Estimated at >$1 Million

Who They Are: Founded in 2000, Local Wine Events is a small, dedicated group that puts together listings for wine tastings and other wine-related events, targeted to specific areas of the country. (Case in point: if you go to the site from a computer in northeastern Indiana, you get "Indianapolis Area Events" right off the bat.) While the number of employees may be modest, however (four in 2009), the site boasts close to 400,000 events[55] listed since its inception and has grown to over 200,000 subscribers already![56]

How They're Doing It: No doubt their growth has benefited from the attention from infamous wine entrepreneur, Gary Vaynerchuk. Gary had owner Eric Orange (@worldwineevents) on his show last year ("Wine Library TV"). Also, "there's an app for that": Apple made Local Wine Events' mobile site a Featured Web App for the iPhone. Finally, Local Wine Events is playing in the Google sandbox as well; they've teamed up with Google Offers for exclusive access to some of the events listed on their site. [57]

All this adds up—to the tune of $250,000 in gross profits for 2009.[58]

But what's even sweeter (like a really, really nice Riesling!) is that those profits don't come from big-ticket hits to YOUR pocket. Want a listing for a single event? It'll cost you a relatively modest $50 (less than you'd pay for decent advertising coverage via print or other media). On the other hand, if your St. Swithin's Day Society has a sip-and-smile to commemorate their patron every July, they can get that recurring listing at a discount. And the best bargain of all? Unlike other publicity ventures, Local Wine Events actually gives you

---

[55] http://www.localwineevents.com/advertise
[56] http://www.localwineevents.com/advertise/eletter
[57] http://www.localwineevents.com/about/press/
[58] http://techcrunch.com/2010/02/21/small-business-spotlight-drink-some-wine-at-local-wine-events/#comment-932433 http://techcrunch.com/2010/02/21/small-business-spotlight-drink-some-wine-at-local-wine-events/#comment-932433

a FREE listing should you opt for such "extras" as videos, ticket processing, or uploading photos.

Where They Came From: A rather circuitous route, actually. Founder Eric Orange has over 20 years in the wine industry, starting from a position as Vineyard Supervisor for Millbrook Vineyards in upstate New York. He's been a wine salesman, a wine steward for private clubs, and achieved first-level certification from the Court of Master Sommeliers during his time as a district manager with Paterno Imports. In all of his roles, one common problem persisted: getting the word out about local wine tastings or wine-centered dinners.

Then, the idea fell into place: instead of scattered individual postings here and there, subject to hit-or-miss coverage, what the industry needed was ONE central site that gathered the information together and made it available with a few mouse clicks. The rest, as the cliché goes, is history…but has a fine bouquet and many promising vintages to come!

Serving Up The Largest E-Commerce Site For Tennis Enthusiasts

Company: Tennis Warehouse
Website: www.tenniswarehouse.com
Last Known Revenue: Undisclosed

Who They Are: Tennis Warehouse is made up of people who love tennis. They love tennis racquets, tennis clothing, and tennis equipment...and they are the leading e-commerce site for those who share that love.

How They're Doing It: Tennis Warehouse has become the largest e-tailer for the tennis industry, offering a full inventory and a unique online racquet demo program. But these tennis-loving folks haven't limited themselves to only one sport, either. Tennis Warehouse has expanded to include Running Warehouse, Skate Warehouse, Tackle Warehouse, Inline Warehouse, Art's Cyclery, Raquetball Warehouse, and Riding Warehouse. If you're looking for a "warehouse" function connected with sports, don't be surprised if you see it in this family sooner rather than later!

Where They Came From: How did Tennis Warehouse successfully climb the ladder of "standing out" from all the other e-tailer behemoths like Amazon? With a focus on service and education. It began in a tiny 500-square-foot tennis shop in the college town of San Luis Obispo, CA, where Drew Munster founded Tennis Warehouse in 1992. He started with a bare-bones, two-page direct-mail catalog. Measly as it was, it listed about half of Tennis Warehouse's inventory at the time. And it still cost him $1,200 to print and mail every two months to 3,000 subscribers. [60]

Searching for an easier (and cheaper!) way, he soon converted to an electronic catalog in which he could list all the products he had at the time—all 200 of them. Without the cumbersome expense of print and mail, then, his largest startup expense for this new format was hiring help to handle e-mail requests for product information. The cost? About $6 per hour, for about 10 hours per week.[59] From e-mail, it was only a short cyber-step for Munster to take to employ the Internet more fully—and build out the software that would come to power Tennis Warehouse.[60]

---

[59] http://www.inc.com/magazine/19960101/1534.html

"Tennis Warehouse really started more or less as a software project for me," he admits. He originally planned to sell the software he'd created for the online version of the Warehouse. However, before long, he realized more people were in love with tennis than with software—and that developing Tennis Warehouse to its full potential would be more lucrative for him.[60]

What tips does Drew have for fledlging entrepreneurs? [60]
- Actively interact with, and listen to, your customers.
- Be an information source for your customers. In the case of tennis, that means helping them understand new technologies, details and specs of racquets, customization, and the thousand other little details that help you rise above the ordinary.
- At all levels, no matter how small, pay attention to the execution of your business. Once again...it's all about the details.

Attention to his customers, his careful expansion, and his myriad "details" has made Drew Munster prosperous—and Tennis Warehouse able to "hold serve" with premier-level e-tailers today.

---

[60]
http://www.racquetsportsindustry.com/articles/2005/11/tennis_warehouse_online_retail.html

From a Modest Start With Coupons to a $90 Million Exit

Company: Retail Me Not (Parent Company is Stateless Systems)
Website: www.retailmenot.com
Last Known Revenue: Estimated at $30 Million (2010)[61]

Who They Are: Australia-based RetailMeNot is online "coupon heaven." Well, okay, sketchy theological reference aside...it's a great place for e-commerce coupons and discount codes, with an estimated 10 million + unique visitors monthly.

How They're Doing It: It's a straightforward sort of thing: the business earns a commission when a consumer uses a coupon from their website to make a purchase online. From an estimated startup cost of a mere $30,[62] RetailMeNot was acquired in 2010 by WhaleShark Media for a whopping $90 Million. Not a bad return for that initial $30![63]

Where They Came From: RetailMeNot was born in October 2006, when Guy King (@GuyKing) and Bevan Clark were frustrated by the flood of websites that promised deals and coupons but didn't deliver. So they decided to build the "better mousetrap" that would bring the world to their door. The initial website took about a week to get up and running, then grew rapidly, thanks in large part to being Google-search friendly.[62]

But another reason for its growth was "good PR"—of the word-of-mouth variety, by customers who knew they'd found something truly different. The difference in RetailMeNot? Guy and Bevan's focus on doing what was best for the consumer, regardless of whether they were able to monetize it. This emphasis on "people before cash" paid off, as RetailMeNot attracted millions of deal-seeking consumers to its website. Millions of *anything* in the online world eventually pays off...and King and Clark monetized those numbers through affiliate partnerships with many of the retailers

---

[61] http://techcrunch.com/2010/12/02/whaleshark-media-closes-a-whale-of-a-financing-buys-retailmenot/
[62] http://www.zdnet.com/from-30-00-to-90-million-retailmenot-1339307735/
[63] http://pulse2.com/2010/12/07/whaleshark-media-acquires-retailnot-com-for-au90-million/

whose coupons they were promoting.[64]

What advice do they have for you? [65]
1. Place user needs before revenue; users will follow, and *that* will bring revenue.
2. Question "traditional" business practices; you just might find a better alternative. Instead of a bevy of software, RetailMeNot uses free online services for email, word processing, spreadsheets, presentations, and accounting.
3. Fail fast, fail often! You learn the most from failures.
4. Build something you'd use yourself.
5. Sometimes, it's better to know "less"—in that you're not hampered by what "you can't do." Prior to Google, many "experts" thought the search arena was pretty well "stitched up" and as good as it was going to get. We all know what happened next!

---

[64] http://www.vistapointadvisors.com/bio-guy-bevan.php
[65] http://startups.sharmavishal.com/2008/12/retailmenotcom-find-share-coupon-codes.html

Personal Services

"A year from now you may wish you had started today." ~Karen Lamb

Converting on an Opportunity to Making Our Memories Last

Company: Scan Digital
Website: www.scandigital.com
Last known revenue: $900,000 (2008)[66]

What They Do: Scan Digital digitizes your old photos and videos to help preserve life's greatest moments. Customers ship their print photos, negatives, VHS, or 8mm videos to Scan Digital headquarters, where the team quickly converts all of your photos and home movies into digital format.

Services start at $.048 per photo and $19.95 per VHS conversion.

How They Do It: Anderson Schoenroch (@AndersonSD) and Michael Mothner (@Mothner), friends from Dartmouth, founded Scan Digital in 2007.   At the time, Anderson was working for Lehman Brothers, and Mothner had started a Web marketing company called Wpromote.

The idea for Scan Digital came one night over Christmas dinner when Mothner's mom, who had just received a digital camera, asked if there was a way that she could digitize all of her old photos stored in her basement. That was the spark the founders needed to realize the potential opportunity for a digital photo scanning service that would help *millions* of Americans preserve their old family photos – by converting them from print to digital.[67]

The founders initially invested $350,000 in the startup, which grossed $200,000 in revenues in its first year. In only its *second* year, revenues were on track to reach a staggering $900,000 – with $569,000 in gross profit. [66]

Repeat business and referrals from satisfied customers account for more than half of the company's revenues. The

---

[66] http://www.inc.com/magazine/20080701/the-get-ahead-guide-scandigital-processes-images.html
[67] http://www.snmag.com/MAGAZINE/Destination-Success/ScanDigital-Co-Founder-Anderson-Schoerock.html

challenge for Scan Digital in growing the company has been in convincing people that shipping their valuable pictures to a remote processing center is safe and secure. To help calm customer fears, Scan Digital maintains an online tracking system that allows customers to follow their photos at every stage in the 14-step fulfillment process.[66]

According to the founders, there were 3 critical factors that played into their decision to launch Scan Digital:

> 1) They validated a need for their service – *everyone* has old photos
> 2) They had nearly *zero* competition, and
> 3) *Of* that competition, all of them severely lacked many of the key things that the team at Scan Digital saw as *critical* to success.

Turns out their vision was correct!

Turbo-Charging Your Career Search!

Company: Venturocket
Website: www.venturocket.com
Last Known Revenue: Undisclosed

Who They Are: Venturocket can be described as the "Google AdWords for Online Job Boards." How are they different from your average job board? Simple: it's called "putting your money where your mouth"—or, in this case, "your ad"—is. Job seekers and employers BOTH spend a bit of cash to get a match...but it's a way better match than you can get by sending your resume and cover letter into the traditional job "black hole" and hoping for the best.

Yes, it's a new concept—and, if the FAQ page is any indication, lots of people are still wrapping their minds around it. But it's an idea whose time has come, and Venturocket's running with it.

How They're Doing It: The steps are simple: if you're seeking a job, you register first, which is free. Then include some billing information and as many skills and expertise keywords as you like, to paint an accurate picture for potential employers of just who you are and what you can do. When an employer signs on to Venturocket, s/he can then peruse the candidates who best match what he or she needs in a potential new employee. If there's a significant match between your skills and the needs of the employer, the employer "buys" your data, and you "buy" the opportunity—and an interview ensues. It streamlines both the candidate-search and job-search processes.

Where They Came From: Marc Hoag (@marchoag), Joe Linn, and Derek Gould are the co-founders, putting together Venturocket in 2011. It sprang from Marc's desire to devise a better job-search engine; like many professionals, he knew résumés, cover letters and typical job descriptions were antiquated and didn't fit the Internet way of searching for a career. After much thought, he reduced the verbiage of résumés, cover letters, and job descriptions to keywords that describe the skills job seekers possess and employers require. The idea of having job-seekers bid on potential careers was a new paradigm—as was the process Marc had to use to build his team. With job- and candidate-search tools that were fast becoming obsolete, Marc filled his team the far better, tried-and-true way: through his personal network.[68]

Where They're Going: Venturocket's fast gaining attention over the Internet...and elsewhere. Daily Tekk has included them in its list of 100 Useful Job & Internship Resources, and they've been invited to compete in the ERE Recruiting Innovation Summit's $10K Startup Competition as well.69 Honors and recognition are great; cash rewards are even better! Venturocket appears to be on its way to garnering both—and changing the way people get their dream jobs in the process.

---

[68] http://techcrunch.com/2011/08/29/venturocket-launches-an-adwords-inspired-jobs-marketplace-to-kill-the-resume/
[69] https://plus.google.com/109847146028268296906/posts/g1Rx4i3iw83

Pay to Have Your Music Critiqued by Famous Musicians and Artists

Company: Blazetrak
Website: www.blazetrak.com
Last Known Revenue: Estimated at <$1 Million[70]

What They Do: Blazetrak is a company which enables independent music artists to post their music making it available to be seen by other musicians as well as to be inspected and edited as well. This is an amazing technique which has modernized the music industry making Blazetrak, no less than miracle workers for bringing the music industry back up to the front of the 21st century marketing world. Blazetrak says this about their product, "Blazetrak is the world's first website that allows you to get directly in touch with established industry experts and celebrity talent - **and be guaranteed a direct video response**."

Depending on the artist or expert, they could charge as little as $100 for their services up to thousands of dollars. But where else in the history of the music industry has this ever been a possibility? Now Musicians can become teachers in their own right.

How'd They Do It: Founded in 2009 by Nathanial Casey (@natecasey), Corey Stanford (@coreyjstanford), Ronald Harrison (@Ron_A_Harrison), and McKinley Joyner, Blazetrak was created as a result of an idea which originated in 2007 mainly when the founders worked at a record company known as Dirty South Records. In order to steer clear from all of the thousands of starving artist submissions which would surely drown their offices, they decided to set up a website which would make it possible for artists to post their music and offer a certain amount of capital in order for their music to be reviewed. They suspected that this would actually cause many musicians who weren't serious to walk away from the record company, leaving more room for the serious talent to come through. This did not end up being the case and within a short amount of

---

[70] http://mashable.com/2011/03/28/blazetrak/

time, thousands of paying customers were asking for their music to be listened to and were willing to pay to do it.[71]

The founders had to work on an efficient model to make it possible to listen to every person who paid for the services which brought them the idea that they needed to create whole new system of marketing for this very concept. Putting this idea to the market they received no less than an astounding level of feedback from musicians and industry leaders.

The response from industry experts and celebrities was also astounding. Chris and Nathanial ended up starting their own business in 2008 which created the separate web site and set up the cash capabilities for Blazetrak. In no time, the two companies brought in enough profit that they were able to redo and develop Blazetrak to become even more efficient and in 2009 the website became open to the public.[71]

---

[71] http://newyorkbuzz.org/2009/11/19/blazetrak-new-site-allows-users-to-submit-demos-and-get-video-feedback-from-a-professional/

Guaranteed Online Dating — Outsourced!

Company: Virtual Dating Assistants
Website: www.virtualdatingassistants.com
Last Known Revenue: Undisclosed

Who Are They? Virtual Dating Assistants (ViDa) is your "date finder," the assistant you wish you had to help you sort out your social life!

What They Do: ViDa says it this way: "The company was founded with one idea in mind: to allow busy singles to fully delegate the online dating process to a team of seasoned experts. We handle the entire online dating process — from choosing the right online dating sites to setting the time, date and location of the first in-person date." (Sounds like everything but picking out the cute shoes or the best tie. There, you're on your own.)[72]

Does it come cheap? Well...not exactly. But then, again, your time's not cheap, either — and are your "date-hunting" results guaranteed? No! I didn't think so. With ViDa working the trenches, on the other hand, you pay $360 to $1,440 per month for *guaranteed* dates — and save your valuable time for other things. (Like picking out those ties and shoes.)

Where They Came From: Founder Scott Valdez (@OutsourceDating) was a lot like many singles— he had a particularly difficult time connecting with women — before one day in 2008, when he decided to try a unique experiment.

First, he hired a personal assistant. Then, he put that assistant through the paces of how to evoke emotion, rate responses, and create an online image so attractive that it made a personal, face-to-face meeting irresistible (and inevitable). Combining that training with a good idea of Scott's taste in women, the assistant then began coordinating Valdez's online dating activity; while Valdez

---

[72] http://www.virtualdatingassistants.com/about-us/

cooked up business deals, his assistant set up the "recipes" for great off-duty social time.[72]

Eighteen amazing dates — and a fistful of eager inquiries from friends about his "experiment" — later, Valdez realized he wasn't the only one who could benefit from a service like this. *Voilá!* Virtual Dating Assistants was launched, and has gained momentum ever since. [72]

One Man's Junk Is Another's Gold Mine

Company: 1-800 Got Junk
Website: www.1800gotjunk.com
Last Known Revenue: $90 Million CDN (2010)[73]

Who They Are: If you've got junk, you need to know these people! 1-800-Got-Junk takes away the stuff consumers and businesses don't want, all over the U.S., Canada, and Australia.

How They're Doing It: More than a little ingenuity, actually. From humble beginnings—one used pickup truck, purchased for $700— they've grown to over 200 franchise locations and have become the "go-to" guys for junk removal...and recycling. Since one man's junk is another man's "find," they recycle a host of items including such hard-to-recycle goods as electronics and appliances in addition to the normal papers, plastics, and metals. Whenever possible, usable goods are donated to charities as well.[74]

Where They Came From: One hungry day in Vancouver, British Columbia, student Brian Scudamore was in the drive-thru at McDonald's and saw a junk-hauling truck ahead of him. By the time he'd snagged his lunch, Scudamore had picked up a business idea as well. (Otherwise known as, "I can do THAT.")

He bought a truck, christened his fledgling business "The Rubbish Boys," and even adopted a slogan: "We'll stash your trash in a flash." Word spread to other students who wanted to pick up some extra cash along with trash, so Brian began hiring others to spread the workload. They even did "junk patrols," cruising the alleys for stuff the city wouldn't take away.[75]

By 1993, a year and a half short of graduation, Brian was ready to "junk" his university plans and quit to concentrate on his business full-time. First, he incorporated the operation as The Rubbish Boys Disposal Service, Inc. By 1999, with locations in Toronto and Portland, OR, however, he changed the name to 1-800-GOT-JUNK

[73] http://en.wikipedia.org/wiki/1-800-GOT-JUNK%3F
[74] http://entrepreneurs.about.com/od/casestudies/a/1800gotjunk.htm
[75] http://www.1800gotjunk.com/us_en/about/our_company.aspx

and wanted to begin franchising. Only one problem...the actual 1-800-GOT-JUNK telephone number was already taken.[75]

Did that stop Scudamore? Hardly. With the drive that made treasure out of city-rejected trash, the enterprising entrepreneur waged a strategic campaign to get the number from the other business. (Well, okay, the "strategic campaign" consisted of begging and pleading. But you get the idea.) After several (dozen? hundred? He's not saying...) calls to the business that had the GOT JUNK number, he clearly made his case well—because he ended up getting that number transferred for FREE.[76]

Thus Scudamore has proceeded, in true bootstrapping fashion—and the more "junk" people have, the better he likes it!

---

[76] http://sprouter.com/blog/brian-scudamore-turned-other-peoples-junk-successful-business/

$200 + a Bicycle = Help for Panicked Electronics Owners!

Company: Geek Squad
Website: www.geeksquad.com
Last Known Revenue: $1-$1.5 Billion (2012)[77]

Who They Are: It'd be tough to find anyone who owns electronics of any sort and doesn't know who the Geek Squad is. You can see their orange-and-black VW bugs driving all over town, even some considerable distances out of "town," as they get dispatched to fix computers and electronics.

How They're Doing It: This group of Geeks, now part of Best Buy, provides consumers with technical support on all things electronic. Computer catch a virus? Geek Squad will send a "Geek" to your home to repair it. They don't wear tights and a cape, but to many a panicked customer, they're superheroes just the same!

Where They Came From: In a word, "starvation." Robert Stephens (@rstephens) founded the Geek Squad after dropping out of the University of Minnesota at age 24, with $200 in his pocket, a bicycle, and a nerdy white-shirt-black-clip-on-tie outfit. He had the idea that pulling up on his bike dressed like a "geek" would inspire a weird confidence in his one-man computer fix-it business among people who were freaking out over their latest crash. [78]

As he found balancing school and business increasingly hard to do, he finally left school and found a startup site in the Warehouse District of Minneapolis, with himself as the only employee. [79]

The company had no advertising budget, so Stephens got creative. He'd drive the Geek Squad car to press events; there's even mention of the Geek Squad logo being imprinted on the soles of his shoes, so when he walked in

---

[77] http://www.marketingshow.com/robert-stephens-geek-squad-best-buy/
[78] http://www.twincities.com/ci_20120887/geek-squad-founder-robert-stephens-leaving-best-buy
[79] http://www.mndaily.com/2007/09/11/geek-squad-founder-named-entrepreneur-year

the snow...voila! As for marketing and advertising itself, Stephens claims the lack of a "budget" actually did them a favor: "Geek Squad had to stand out because we couldn't afford to be in the Yellow pages, we couldn't afford to have billboards, we couldn't afford to have TV..." [77]

"That way you end up with a more authentic brand rather than a contrived one, which does not inspire anyone but the CEO,"[79] he said.

What does he tell students and others looking for a winning direction in business? "You've got to be a Da Vinci. I believe everybody is a genius at something, not everything. People are going to have to reach inside themselves and find out where they're going to be great at and what do they want to be great at. And here's the hint. It's what you'd probably do even if you didn't get paid at it anyway. It's the thing that gets you out of bed at two in the morning and you get that notebook next to your bed, and you wake up and you write ideas, and you're always thinking about it. That's probably where you're meant to be in the world."[77]

Nowadays, the Geeks are everywhere...and happy Best Buy (and other) customers continue to rely on them for every day tech support at home and in the office.

Business Services and Software

*"By the way, what have you done that's so great?
Do you create anything, or just criticize other's work
and belittle their motivations?"* ~ Steve Jobs

Company: 37signals
Website: www.37signals.com
Last known revenue: Estimated at $8 million (2008)[80]

What They Do: 37signals is a web application and software design company offering easy-to-use small business tools for project management, customer relations, and business productivity.

They charge anywhere from $12 to $149 per month for their products, but unlike *most* software-as-a-service companies, they do not offer any free versions of their products. Their products have been praised time and time again by customers and the media, for their products' simplicity and quality, as well as for co-founder Jason Fried's business theories and practices.

How They're Doing It: 37signals was founded as a Web design firm in Chicago in 1999, by Jason Fried (@jasonfried), Carlos Segura (@SeuguraInc), and Ernest Kim (@edotkim). It quickly transitioned into a web application development company, by building its flagship project management software, BaseCamp. 37signals has been a premium case study for entrepreneurs and software developers alike, for their ability to succeed through their focus on simplicity. Their suite of 5 products often have far fewer features than their competitors, but their ability to focus on building the *right* features, the right *way*, has helped propel them into the spotlight of success.

Jason Fried has now published two popular books that cover his product development best practices: *Rework* and *Getting Real*, and he has been named one of the **Top 35 Innovators in the World Under 35** by *MIT Technology Review*.

With just over 20 employees, 37signals has stayed close to its roots and is reportedly extremely profitable due to their low overhead costs and scalable business model.

---

[80] http://webdevnews.net/2009/03/basecamp-37signals-ror-one-of-web-20s-best-start-up-businesses/

One thing Fried and the team at 37signals have been disciplined about, is creating supremely valuable products that customers pay for, and doing so without offering a freemium model (free versions of software). Fried has been quoted as saying, "The idea of giving away products is "truly insane!" and that he'd, "*much* rather serve a smaller, pay-only customer base than a large, unwieldy—and possibly unprofitable—one."[81]

Fried and his team took risks with the belief that, if something is good enough, you don't have to give out samples; people will gladly pay for great products – especially user-friendly products!

[81] http://www.inc.com/magazine/20101101/go-ahead-raise-your-businesss-prices.html

Helping Freelancers Get Paid

Company: FreshBooks
Website: www.freshbooks.com
Last Known Revenue: Undisclosed

What They Do: FreshBooks is an online invoicing service that makes managing client billing & invoicing easy and painless for freelancers and small businesses. With tools that make it easy to track billable hours, organize multiple client projects, and improved project managing software, FreshBooks has managed over $1 Billion in client transactions to date for its customers.[82]

FreshBooks offers packages starting for free for a basic package up to a $39.95 per month package that offers an unlimited number of clients, unbranded emails, and more advanced expense reporting tools.

How They're Doing It: Mike McDerment (@MikeMcDerment) and Joe Sawada, co-founders, launched FreshBooks in May of 2004. At the time they met, Mike was running a design firm and hired Joe as a contractor. It would turn out to be a lucrative decision.[83]

The initial FreshBooks application was intended to provide online time-tracking as well as a simple invoicing service for freelancers like Mike. Mike used the cash flow that was coming in from his consulting business to help fund FreshBooks. He continued to financially nurse their baby until it became cash-flow-positive on its own. [83]

From day one, FreshBooks spent their money on advertising by focusing on targeted niches and on direct-response marketing in email newsletters. Their experience with a PR firm left them with a sour taste in their collective mouths, so they soon decided to focus on direct marketing and advertising. It proved to be a successful avenue, as it became their most successful customer acquisition channel.

---

[82] http://techcrunch.com/2010/07/14/in-five-months-freshbooks-crosses-1-billion-in-transactions/

Mike's background was in SEO. We'll go out on a limb here and guess that likely didn't hurt either. [83]

Mike admits that, "the technology and app development is the easy part. The hard part about building and scaling a web business is the marketing and customer acquisition."[83]

Their story proves that if you have a good idea, a good market for it, and a firm belief that what you provide is an excellent product, it takes little more than hard work, patience, research and focus. Seeing a trend here?

[83] http://mixergy.com/freshbooks-mike-mcderment/

2 Founders Develop Analytical Software Better Than Google

Company: Clicky
Website: www.getclicky.com
Last Known Revenue: Estimated at $1 Million + (2010)[84]

Who They Are: Clicky is two-person company that is actually able to compete with Google in the analytical software area. It's a real-time Web analytics platform that offers detail on website visitors to help businesses better understand who's coming to their websites, and how — *immediately*. [84]

How They're Doing It: Used in some capacity by over 500,000 websites, Clicky differentiates itself from Google Analytics in that it's a paid service. Monthly plans start at $9.95 for up to 10 websites, and $29.95 for 40 websites. They also earn revenue from both advertising and a white-label analytics solution for other service providers such as Webs.com (a source that makes it easy for individuals to create their own websites).

Clicky's prime advantage over most other analytics is its real-time, up-to-the-minute capabilities. This means, for example, that if a business has an article hit the front page of a popular site like digg.com, they'll see the traffic spike in Clicky immediately, along with links back to the sources sending that traffic. This enables companies to be flexible, adaptable, and "turn on a dime" to make adjustments in their website reach and visibility.

Where They Came From: Noah Merritt and Sean Hammons (@schammy) were business partners who had already dabbled in highly focused search engine databases when they put together NowTowns out of Corvallis, OR, in 2004. Ironically, NowTowns didn't take off as they hoped—but in the process of building custom Web tracking for it, the concept of Clicky came to them. They put together Clicky with affiliate marketing to generate leads and sales, which

---

[84] http://mixergy.com/noah-merritt-clicky-interview/

allowed the founders to pay only if they got a new customer signed on.[84]

What would they do differently? One major thing: changing the pricing structure so they wouldn't have shortchanged themselves at the beginning. Co-founder Sean Hammons explains that Clicky really didn't charge enough for their services at the beginning.

Bootstrappers can often get a bit sensitive about asking a premium price for what they do. Sean advises, this is actually **"a huge mistake."[85] He urges entrepreneurs not to be afraid of this—after all, most people still do believe you "get what you pay for."**

Despite this early misstep, however, Clicky is successfully competing with Google in the analytics game—to the tune of generating a 60% profit margin and over $1 million in revenues. People are getting what they're paying for with Clicky...and, apparently, loving the end result.[84]

---

[85] http://www.retireat21.com/interview/sean-hammons-founder-of-getclickycom

Programmers + Collaboration...Who Knew?

Company: Github
Website: www.github.com
Last Known Revenue: Undisclosed

Who They Are: Github is a social network for programmers (yes, you heard that right—even if "programmers" and "social" don't seem to fit in the same sentence...) that makes it possible for teams to work and collaborate on software code. Go figure! And lots of people do just that: Github has been used by over a million people to create and share code.[86]

How They're Doing It: In a word—inexpensively. Github premium plans start at $7/month for individuals—that's a *premium* plan, folks. When was the last time you got anything "premium" for $7?—and go up as far as $200 for a business account. This provides more private repositories where business programmers can upload development code for collaboration.

Where They Came From: Remember that old line on your report card about "plays well with others"? Well, that's what Chris Wanstrath (@defunkt), PJ Hyett (@PJHyett), and Tom Preston-Werner (@mojombo) wanted to do, but they were programmers without an acceptable means of sharing code. So, one day in 2008, they simply started making up their own.[86]

At first, Github was a weekend project, a piece-by-piece build to which they devoted their Saturdays. They'd start in the morning with food, of course—what genuine creativity can happen without that?—and then divide and conquer the tasks at hand. Tom designed the pages or features and Chris implemented them. Then, they'd test Github out at the "day job"—which was also a startup Chris had founded with PJ. Day by day, test by test, this became a great proving ground; what's better than "real world" use to find out which elements of a system work and which don't?[87]

---

[86] http://www.wired.com/wiredenterprise/2012/02/github/all/1
[87] http://37signals.com/svn/posts/2486-bootstrapped-profitable-proud-github

Eventually, it was time to let the new puppy out—in a controlled backyard. So they did, via a free public launch that Chris, Tom, and PJ set up in beta form for their friends. From there, however, the puppy took a figurative quantum leap over the fence. People loved it. They could create public OR private repositories for free—what's not to love about that?—and, in a flash, they were using it for their businesses' codes. This wasn't a surprise, considering Chris and PJ had already done just that! With a few (dozen!) e-mails from friends asking how they could set up paid, private repositories...Github became a going concern.[87] And it's going strong to this day!

NOTE: During the publication of this book, Github received $100 Million in venture capital from Andreessen Horowitz. Github has previously prided itself on its ability to bootstrap itself to profitability and grow 300% annually.[88]

---

[88] http://gigaom.com/2012/07/09/github-finally-raises-funding-100m-from-andreessen-horowitz/

One-Stop Payroll and Human Resources Management...Online

Company: Paycom
Website: www.paycomonline.com
Last Known Revenue: $42.6 Million (2010)[89]

Who They Are: Paycom is the nation's fastest-growing payroll company, offering full-service online payroll processing and human resources information. They serve businesses of all sizes who want a more efficient, less expensive way to manage key payroll and HR responsibilities — things like payroll processing and employee time and attendance, as well as human resource information such as applicant tracking, background checks, benefits and COBRA administration.

How They're Doing It: With dedicated Payroll Specialists and pay-as-you-go pricing, Paycom takes the hassle out of maintaining employee records of all sorts. Businesses enter the information once for all reports—no duplication of effort. The 24/7 availability of help and access from anywhere you have an Internet connection...well, those are just gravy. And the "gravy" doesn't come with any hidden surprises, either: businesses don't have to purchase new software, secure licenses, or fret about annual price increases. They pay for the services they use, and those services are more convenient to manage than ever before.

Where They Came From: Paycom began in 1998, founded by Chad Richison, who began his career in the payroll industry and soon found himself wanting to venture into online payroll services. So he did, using a combination of his personal savings, a SBA loan, and 11 credit cards![90] When Paycom launched, it was the first 100% online payroll services provider—and it hasn't taken long for companies to latch onto that convenience. Catering to the increasing numbers of industries that outsource what used to be in-house operations and taking advantage of the ease of using the "cloud" for such services, Paycom has taken off like a

---

[89] http://www.inc.com/inc5000/profile/paycom
[90] http://www.inc.com/inc5000/profile/paycom

shot: Richison himself was a finalist in the Ernst & Young's Entrepreneur Of The Year® Awards Program[91] and was ranked 1,814 on *Inc.com's* 5000 list in 2011.[90]

When asked about taking the "plunge" into a new venture, Richison offers prospective entrepreneurs some sage advice.[92]

1.) Line up the right financing by using some of your personal savings and getting a loan from the SBA.
2.) Know your customers and know your market.
3.) Stay determined and don't focus on the future too much in the beginning.

Focusing on the present—on present customers' payroll and human resources needs—works for Paycom, to the tune of almost $43 million; managing data on the "cloud" apparently means "the sky is the limit"!

---

[91] http://www.i-newswire.com/paycom-ceo-chad-richison-named/36459
[92] http://www.growinokc.com/index.php?src=gendocs&ref=ChadRichison&category=OKCSucc essStories&submenu=ChadRichison

From A One-Man Startup to Millions...In Three Years or Less!

Company: Balsamiq Studios
Website: www.balsamiq.com
Last Known Revenue: Estimated at >$2 Million (2011) [94]

Who They Are: Balsamiq is a software company whose flagship product, "Mockups," makes it easy for software designers and developers to build great software by letting them easily sketch out (i.e., wireframe) their ideas, then quickly collaborate and iterate over them.

Balsamiq's monthly plans start out at $12/month for those smaller projects and up to $249 for up to 100 projects. [93]

How They're Doing It: Profitably, indeed. As a one-man software startup, it accumulated $4,432 in revenue in only its third week of existence. In less than five months, it hit $100K, and by the "toddler" stage of 18 months, the Balsamiq "baby" had crossed the $2 million line — of which almost half is pure profit![94] Balsamiq alone has netted over $2 million in total sales in first 18 months of business and is gathering momentum at breakneck speed [94]

Where They Came From: Giacomo "Peldi" Guilizzoni (@peldi), the founder of Balsamiq, experienced firsthand the challenges of sketching and collaborating on new mock-ups while working as a programmer at Adobe, where the standard was PowerPoint for wireframing. That's when he got the "aha" moment for Balsamiq. But, to mutilate an old saying, there's many a slip 'twixt company idea and celebratory champagne sip: it took him close to eight months of working from 8:00 to midnight, every day, to make the launch succeed. [94]

But many an entrepreneur puts in those kinds of hours; that's not unusual. How did Balsamiq grow so fast as a one-man show? Surprisingly enough — perhaps counter-intuitively enough — *not* through a lot of advertising and paid marketing. In fact, Peldi spent $0 on marketing and/or advertising at launch.

---

[93] http://www.balsamiq.com/buy
[94] http://mixergy.com/balsamiq-peldi-guilizzoni-interview/

What did he do instead? He used the marketing savvy of the 21st century: blogging himself and sending e-mail invites to 40 other influential bloggers. Peldi would also search for blogs and forums talking about wire framing and gently let the audience know about Balsamiq as a solution to meet their needs.

The other side of the coin was the quality product, and Balsamiq is above all known for their class-act product, built on simplicity and usability, not features, which has won over many, *many* fans.[94]

Early users (aka Evangelists) were given free access to Balsamiq and in return for a great experience, those evangelists spread the good word about Balsamiq to their peers and colleagues. The good word spread around fast and soon enough Peldi was able to put up his paywall and see those profits start rolling int.[94]

Here's to proving that simple can be done successfully. Well done Peldi!

Time and Expense Tracking without Tears

Company: Replicon
Website: www.replicon.com
Last Known Revenue: $20M (2011)[95]

Who They Are: Replicon is a company that provides SaaS (Software as a Service) <u>timesheet</u> and expense management software you can use to automate tracking employee and project time, expenses, and resource schedules—and they're one of Canada's Best Places To Work!

How They're Doing It: With speed and spirit. They're recognized as one of the fastest-growing technology companies out there (besides being a ball to work at, as above), and they scored a finalist's spot for the Ernst & Young Entrepreneur Award.[96]

Where They Came From: Raj Narayanaswamy and Lakshmi Raj started Replicon in 1996, when they quit jobs at software companies to start a new venture financed in part by $80k - $90k of credit card debt and part by dipping into their personal savings.[97]

Replicon's first product was a product called Reach, a help desk product. Being featured on Netscape brought them early success, which encouraged them to launch three new products. Unfortunately, however, it may have been a case of too much too fast: those products never achieved the success that Reach did, and before long, Raj and Lakshmi knew they had serious problems. Fast going broke, they went out on consulting jobs as an attempt to keep both themselves and their company afloat.

And then...serendipity ensued.

---

[95] http://www.sramanamitra.com/2011/07/15/bootstrapping-to-20m-replicon-co-founders-raj-and-lakshmi-narayanaswamy-part-1/
[96] http://www.replicon.com/awards-and-recognition
[97] http://mixergy.com/raj-and-lakshmi-replicon-interview/

Consultants and freelancers often spend way too many hours managing time and expense sheets for their clients...in fact, it is a royal headache. But, just as Newton discovered great science out of a headache from a fallen apple, Raj and Lakshmi looked at each other across the expense-sheet mess and had an "aha" moment. What the world needed was a better way to manage all that detail![97]

So they began working the "moonlight shift," consulting by day, feverishly devising a new product by night—often until 3 A.M. This didn't make consulting by day any easier, but it soon paid off in a product they knew would solve a problem—after all, they'd be their own first customers! [97]

This time, too, they proceeded with a slightly different mode of promoting and marketing. This time, they didn't put all their eggs only in the Netscape basket; some of those eggs, they gave away—a free version of the product that customers could try before they sprung for all the "bells, horns, and whistles." [97]

That idea? Solid gold: within three weeks, they had their first customer who paid $3,000 for the full version.[98] That company had 100 employees, each of whom paid $29 per license to use the timesheet software...and Raj and Lakshmi no longer teetered at the edge of financial disaster. In fact, that sale enabled them to keep their heads above water long enough to get Replicon back on its feet—and get themselves some sleep!

You might say Replicon's been going "swimmingly" ever since—and companies everywhere thank Replicon for helping their employees not lose sleep over tracking detail!

Proving Why Niche Can Equal Riches

Company: Ubertor
Website: www.ubertor.com
Last Known Revenue: >$1 Million (2011)[99]

Who They Are: Ubertor just may be a realtor's best friend: they offer premium, video-enhanced website templates to help real estate agents build and customize their own websites and real estate listings.

How They're Doing It: With charges that range from $17 to $129 per month for their suite of professional website templates, Ubertor is fast-growing and profitable. One of their keys? Outsourcing. When they kept their operations Stateside, their results were modest at best. However, partnering with a labor force in the Philippines has enabled Ubertor to truly "take off." Today the company grosses more than $1 million in revenues, out of which the founders indicate a profit of a "few hundred thousand."[99]

Where They Came From: Stephen Jagger (@sjagger) and high school buddy Mike Stevenson (@WhistlerMike) co-founded Ubertor "accidentally," according to Jagger. They'd initially co-founded a Web hosting company, but quickly found that the pressure to make their prices competitive (translate: cheap) in that industry were squeezing all their potential profits away. [99]

Then one of their Web hosting clients, a real estate agent, asked them if they could help him build a website to manage his real estate listings. At the time, a real estate agent had to ask his/her Web developer to upload and update new listings—pretty "old school"! But from that "old-school" approach came a light bulb moment...one they could run with. [99]

Jagger knew that real estate agents were willing to pay for help with websites and online visibility. Not only that; their unique needs in terms of highlighting their listings weren't being adequately covered with the available Web templates of the day. That's where Ubertor found its niche—when it set out to solve that Web problem and cater specifically to a real estate niche. [99]

---

[99] http://mixergy.com/stephen-jagger-ubertor-interview/

As with many Bootstrappers, the co-founders made their fair share of sacrifices—living with their parents, working other odd jobs (even bar bouncers) to keep cash coming in. But soon enough, they were able to show real estate agents a Web presence tailored to their needs.[99] The rest, as they say in "old school" terms, was history.

Now, Ubertor is the place realtors are "SOLD" on for one major reason: it's the Web "location, location, location" for their specific niche and serving their specific needs—for "uber" success!

Productivity Software for your Business...Direct from the Cloud!

Company: Zoho
Website: www.zoho.com
Last Known Revenue: $40 Million (2008)[100]

Who They Are: If you need a myriad of software applications to help your business be more productive and efficient, you want to know Zoho. They offer business productivity applications, from CRM solutions like Salesforce to project management. In short, if you need help getting things done, Zoho's who you ought to be calling!

How They're Doing It: At the very least, your business may well PAY the very least: Zoho is famous for offering versions of their software for free, or at greatly (as in HUGELY) reduced prices compared with their competitors. Even businesses that need software for multiple users get a break: for you, Zoho sells its software on a monthly basis.

But where Zoho truly shines is in what they've done about a company's need for ANY software...at all.

"We are trying to be the IT department for these small and medium (sized) businesses," Vembu says. "We're trying to create a portfolio of products so that businesses can pay a monthly fee, like a utility bill, and get all the software they need."[101]

As a result, for almost any item of software your enterprise may require, Zoho has now created an online alternative. From e-mail to word processing, calendars to spreadsheets, conferencing to customer relationship management, project management tools to presentation binders and more: it's all covered by one monthly fee.

Where They Came From: While the company itself has been around for over a decade, the present incarnation of Zoho didn't come into being until 2005. In 2003, the company's only business was network management software, a small source of success and profits. But when Indian entrepreneur Sridhar Vembu looked around, he was concerned about Zoho having too many eggs in just one basket—

---

100 http://www.labnol.org/tech/zoho-revenues/12497/

101 http://blogs.zoho.com/why-we-haven-t-taken-venture-capital/

depending too much on a few large clients. At the time, Zoho was also a customer of Salesforce, but felt it was overpriced.[102]

As a software engineer, Sridhar felt they could build a better product; as an entrepreneur, he wanted to make his own mark on the Salesforce model and offer the product at a better price. "From my perspective," he says, "all this had the added merit that we would target small and mid-sized customers first, which would let us avoid the long sales cycles and the politics. That was just a thought, an idea, without yet a plan of action."[103]

It didn't take long for a plan of action to materialize.

Zoho began its bootstrapping endeavor with one initial application, a primitive online word processor called Zoho Writer, in 2005. At the time, the company did Writer "on the side"; what was true then, and is still true today, is that the company's real revenue came from its network management software for enterprises. Then Google acquired a program called Writely, which it transformed into Google Docs. Overnight, the world realized that browser-based software could handle tasks like word processing...and Zoho Writer took off like a shot.

And as far as challenging Salesforce at its own game? Looks like that's working rather well, too. Today, Zoho CRM is the fastest growing part of the Zoho suite—turning a nice profit AND giving Salesforce a run for its money. Sridhar adds, "Zoho CRM also paved the way to our emergence as one of the most comprehensive suite of business applications in the cloud. I guess we should thank StorageTek."[104]

Today, Zoho is 600 employees strong in India and does $40 Million+ in revenues each year—out of which it turns a nifty $12 Million+ in profits.[105] Clearly, being in charge of the Next Big Thing is a great place to be: Sridhar says he turns down an average of three venture capitalist and/or private equity deals every week from investors who want a piece of Zoho's success. But this entrepreneur is in no

---

102 http://mixergy.com/Sridhar-vembu/

103http://m.xconomy.com/3376/show/0eb429bf24dec3bf6a69de998432b77e&t=0a472e9fc7988e94a181cf606ee70916

104 http://www.zoho.com/general/blog/how-a-cancelled-project-at-storagetek-led-to-zoho-crm.html

105 http://www.forbes.com/2008/02/22/mitra-zoho-india-tech-inter-cx_sm_0222mitra.html

hurry to stray from his bootstrapped roots and, as of this writing, is "working the cloud" without any outside capital involved!

Launching With 2 Children and a Full-time Job

Company: Sticky Albums
Website: www.stickyalbums.com
Last Known Revenue: Estimated at ~$100,000

Who They Are: StickyAlbums is a site where photographers win two ways: they get a mobile app with which to share their photos with friends and family—AND they get exposure and a new revenue channel. It's darned near a "picture perfect" opportunity!

How They're Doing It: StickyAlbums has monthly plans for photographers starting at $27 per month and annual plans going up to $997—which gives a user an unlimited number of mobile albums to give or sell to their clients. Today, StickyAlbums has over 1,500 customers, a success rate its founder attributes to the idea's simplicity.

Where They Came From: Founder Nate Grahek (@stickyalbums) from Minneapolis was working full-time for a large education company, raising one child with another one due. On the side, he did amateur photography, mostly family portraits. When his clients asked Nate how they could get their professional photos on their mobile phones to share with friends and review which photos they wanted to print, he realized that providing wallet-print photos as samples had lost its impact and effectiveness in the digital age. What people needed were "wallet prints" that were digital.[106]

Grahek used his limited programming skills to create a very basic app that enabled him to manually upload photos, then give that URL to his clients, who could in turn then view and share photos from their mobile phones. The app was such a hit that he decided to create online training videos teaching other photographers how to build the same app.   Fortunately, however, he had a neighbor who was a software engineer—and talked him out of the idea of expecting busy photographers to watch videos teaching them the process he could do *for* them![106]

To test the idea, he ran a promotion in a popular blog for $500: a contest that offered his app in exchange for a free blog post, to test his website and see if photographers would pay for his service. The

---

[106] http://www.marketingshow.com/nate-grahek-stickyalbums-interview/

contest worked, netting him 25 clients who began uploading unlimited albums for Nate to process on the back end. That became "good news, bad news" for Grahek: clearly, photographers liked the idea—but just as clearly, doing the process himself was far too time-intensive. [106]

The next step? The manual process had to give way to an automated one. But how to do that?

Grahek decided to look into hiring a programmer and got quotes in the range of $10 to $20K to develop the automation app, but he wasn't quite ready to risk the farm. So once again, he tested the idea. He ran another a promotion for his service in a popular photography blog; this time, he got 189 clients to sign on. Their fees added up to nearly $20,000—enough to give him the capital he needed to farm out development of what would become StickyAlbums. [106]

As soon as he started making money, he also outsourced non-core activities such as graphic design and marketing to freelancers. This gave him the leverage he needed to balance his full-time job, family, and fast-growing startup. The one thing he kept personal control of was customer support; in his view, being close to his customers was his most important job. [106]

Today, Grahek says his success comes from having something new that photographers could resell to their clients. He didn't offer them just a new version of something they did already, or merely a new website. StickyAlbums became an entirely new revenue channel —and one that differentiated its users from other photographers. [106]

The only question people still ask is, how did he find the time to launch a startup with a full-time job, a wife, a child, and one another on the way? The answers are what you might expect: lots of late nights—and cutting out such time-wasters as too much TV and "playing" on the Internet. [106] StickyAlbums has become the best use of the Internet he could have imagined...and the picture of its future is indeed bright!

Buffing and Polishing the Digital Legal Document Business

Company: Logik
Website: www.logik.com
Last Known Revenue: $4.4 Million (2008)[107]

Who They Are: Logik is a company that helps businesses organize and process digital legal documents. Yes, that's right: digital documents. As in eliminating mountains and mountains of paper. What's not to love?

How They're Doing It: Andy Wilson (@iDedupde) and Sheng Yang set up what would become Logik in Andy's dining room and financed their beginnings by tapping into their savings and running up their credit-card balances! From an initial capitalization of less than $20,000,[108] Logik landed their first client, which brought in $45,000.[108]

Where They Came From: Andy and Sheng were fellow Hokies at Virginia Tech in 2004, working for a small legal printing company, and dumbfounded at the sheer amount of paper being schlepped from office to office, from locale to locale, across the country—for routine legal proceedings. Truckloads of it went out every day, for nothing more than to be stored for safekeeping. So much else in the business world was becoming purely electronic that they couldn't help wondering...why not legal documentation? Seeing the need for large-scale electronic data processing, the duo put their heads together to create the software to handle it. [108]

First, they drew out the process flow for the proposed software. Then they took the giant leap of quitting their day jobs, cut expenses to the bone, leased some servers, and went to work. They had reason for optimism: Andy has a Computer Science background, while Sheng is an engineer—as it turned out, an ideal combination to build the Logik solution. It took nine months for that first client to come through, but since then, Logik has been profitable— and growing ever since.[109]

---

[107] http://www.inc.com/inc5000/profile/logik
[108] http://37signals.com/svn/posts/2385-bootstrapped-profitable-proud-logik

Revenues have climbed steadily, from $373,866 in 2005 to $4.4 million in 2008—out of which $3 million was profit—with just 8 employees.[108] This synergistic mix of hard work, good luck, and meeting a clear need put them on the *Inc.* 500 list in 2009, as one of the fastest-growing private companies in the country.[107] Logik's a perfect small-business success story: Determine a need, fill it...and make money. In other words, entrepreneurship at its best.

[109] http://logik.com/about/our_story/

"Actions, Not (Just) Page Views" — A Profitable Difference

Company: FoxMetrics
Website: www.foxmetrics.com
Last Known Revenue: Undisclosed

Who They Are: FoxMetrics has created what could be called a "premium version" of Google Analytics: a sophisticated web analytics, SEO, and social media monitoring tool for businesses that aggregates analytics for companies into one platform. Numbers, people, actions, trends, preferences...it's all there. Data, collected, analyzed and put together in a form that YOU can use.

How They're Doing It: It depends on what you want and need. You can go with "just the facts, Ma'am"—a basic plan—for as little as $20/month. From their most popular "professional"-level plan will run approximately $60/month, you can select from various pricing structures all the way to "the works" —a high-volume "enterprise plan" that comes with a year's contract, covering heavy-duty numbers, advanced analytics and features.

FoxMetrics encourages its clients to continue to use any combination of analytics tools already in place for tracking raw data such as page views and the like. Then, with FoxMetrics, you can go further: take that data and examine your visitors' purposes, demographics, and other more detailed information. As they explain on their site, *"Once we've received data from you regarding your customers and their actions — you can slice and dice the data from within your dashboard as you see fit...starting from creating segments, funnels, ad-hoc reports, real-time drill downs and more."*[110]

Where They Came From: Indirectly, from Sierra Leone—that's founder Rydal Williams' country of origin. Wanting to make an impact in his industry, he dug around, got below "skin deep" and found out a key need in the marketplace...one he could fill. As he put it, "We found out

---

[110] http://foxmetrics.com/Docs

that most, if not all, Web analytics users have to sign up for multiple tools just to get a complete insight into the interactions of their web audience."[111]

So the obvious question presented itself: why make customers use a whole toolbox's worth of "stuff" if one tool would do? Voilá! Answering that question proved to be a key to his next steps.

"After researching business opportunities," he says, "we decided to launch a Web analytics tool because we have experience in implementing and using the top-tier Web analytics solutions that are available to Fortune 500 companies. We also have significant experience with other mainstream analytics tools such as Google Analytics, MixPanel, KISSMetrics, Omniture, CoreMetrics and more."[111]

In other words—Rydal took the power of high-end enterprise-level applications, tweaked with real-time and custom event tracking added...and ended with practical, straightforward data in one place, convenient and centralized. That's the FoxMetrics advantage!

---

[111] http://foxmetrics.com/blog/What-is-FoxMetrics-5

Demonstrating That Simpler Sometimes Means Better

Company: Team Gantt
Website: www.teamgantt.com
Last Known Revenue: Estimated at $500,000

Who They Are: TeamGantt is a super- simple project scheduler using the foundations of Gantt charts to manage projects and to keep them on time. So what makes them different? While there are plenty of project management software solutions out there, Team Gantt cut through the noise by focusing on simplicity and building the best apps to cover the basic needs of their customers.

How They're Doing It: With the promise of "easy project scheduling that you and your team will love," TeamGantt makes good on that promise with software that ranges in price from $10 to $79 per month. They have 1,000 paid subscribers from the ranks of the Fortune 500, as well as creatives, event planners, and startups.[112]

Where They Came From: TeamGantt was cofounded in 2009 by John Correlli (@johncorrelli) and long-time pal Nathan Gilmore (@NathanGilmore), after they'd spent a good long time looking for a way to schedule projects online—only to find there wasn't one! In view of that lack, they decided to try to build it themselves. This effort, of course, was in addition to their full-time IT jobs.

"We started working Saturdays in my basement at the end of 2009," Gilmore explains. "I worked on the design, and John would build the app. We started gaining interest and traction right away. We had a beta out in the spring of 2010 and launched officially in November of 2010. [113] By August of 2011, the business grew to the point where we knew that if we really wanted to take things to the next level, we would need to quit our jobs and go full-time with TeamGantt. Since then, the business has taken off."

"We're completely bootstrapped and profitable,"[112] he concludes. "We have had interest from investors, but haven't needed it yet." [112]

---

[112] http://techcrunch.com/2012/07/25/teamgantt-is-a-streamlined-online-project-management-tool/
[113] http://teamgantt.com/about-us/

That's not surprising. In this age of ever-more-complicated lives full of multitasking and crowded schedules, any tool that promises to "keep things simple" will be popular, indeed. TeamGantt's "keeping it simple" approach answers tough project tracking questions with designs that are easy to use, simple…and beautiful. You have their word on it!

Online Marketing

"You're on your own. And you know what you know. And YOU are the guy who'll decide where to go." ~
Dr. Seuss

Proving that Google Adwords Isn't the Only Game in Town

Company: BuySellAds
Website: www.buysellads.com
Last Known Revenue: $1.5M (2008)[114]

What They Do: BuySellAds.com is a direct advertising marketplace serving 2.2 *billion* impressions across roughly 1,500 sites. From 2009 to 2010, they grew 400% and have transformed the way that bloggers and small media sites manage and sell their online ad inventory.

BuySellAds charges a 25% flat fee for the ads sold through its platform and provides an easier way for bloggers to sell direct advertising on their sites to interested advertisers.

How They're Doing It: In 2007, founder Todd Garland (@Toddo) was running two web sites on the side as a hobby, **CSS Elite** and **13 Styles**. Todd was constantly having to manage advertiser relationships and billing, which proved to be a real pain. The idea for BuySellAds was conceived by his frustration of having to manage ad inventory and advertiser billing on his own. He set out to create a platform that would help automate the process and solve his problems at the same time.[115]

BuySellAds has grown mostly through word-of-mouth from satisfied customers. The advantage of having bloggers who use your product is that they will blog about how much they like your product to their *own* audiences. Free advertising from your customers is hard to beat!

Although there are several well-known ad networks out there, Google AdSense being the biggest, BuySellAds isn't directly competing with these other ad networks. Why? Because *their* offering focuses on *direct* advertising relationships, as opposed to *indirect* – like AdSense does.

---

[114] http://www.slideshare.net/toddgarland/buyselladscom-0-to-15-million-in-11-months-while-working-a-9-to-5-todd-garland
[115] http://mixergy.com/buysellads-todd-garland-interview/

BuySellAds, therefore, provides bloggers an alternative solution for a slightly more unique problem.

As you can plainly see here, bigger is *not* always better.

Sure, undertaking a venture that goes up against...well...*anything* with the word "Google" preceding it can be quite the intimidating and daunting task. But Todd didn't let that stop him!

He simply designed what he felt was a better alternative to a common problem. It turns out his feeling was quite mutual.

He made a product and service so good that his customers essentially did the brunt of the marketing *for* him!

Todd is living, breathing proof that if you build it, and build it *better*, they will indeed come!

Proving That Putting Clients First is a Successful Strategy

Company: HubShout
Website: www.hubshout.com
Last known revenue: Undisclosed

Who They Are: HubShout is an Internet marketing software and service provider of online marketing solutions for small and medium-sized businesses. Additionally, HubShout runs a large reseller program that enables other Web design, agency, and advertising consultants to "white-label" their software and offer all of these services under their own brand.

How They're Doing It: Their reseller programs provide website design and marketing companies with all the tools they need to run and manage their own client-driven SEO and PPC advertising campaigns. HubShout's reseller program starts at $199 per month for the basic package and runs up to $325 per month for the full suite.

Where They Came From: HubShout was co-founded by Georgetown MBA grad Chad Hill (@ChadAHill) and Dr. Adam Stetzer. Prior to founding HubShout, Hill led the marketing department for a startup and saw firsthand the struggle digital marketing agencies had with providing the analytics he sought. Hill thought, "I can do better than this!"—and set out to prove it.[117]

His extensive network gave him ten clients right from the get-go; then he brought Stetzer into the fold as a tech guru to help him build OEM software...which became the HubShout we know today. The key difference between HubShout and what had gone before it? It became all about ownership—and labeling. Hill and Stetzer decided that rather than keep the software to themselves, they'd offer it through a white-label program: allow any SEO or Pay-Per-Click agency to re-sell HubShout's software under their own names to their own clients.[116]

What would Hill advise those seeking to start their own SEO or online marketing agency? "Really identify your target market and

---

[116] http://www.prnewswire.com/news-releases/hubshout-wins-best-in-search-award-162795486.html

your sales channel, because there is so much demand that it is hard to be a generalist."

He goes on to remind Bootstrappers not to put the proverbial cart before the horse: **Only after you figure out your target market, ideal customer, and your niche should you worry about your brand, logo, and such.**[117]

---

[117] http://hubshout.com/?How-to-start-an-SEO-business&AID=858

"Designing" a Showplace for Creativity

Company: Carbonmade
Website: www.carbonmade.com
Last Known Revenue: Undisclosed

Who Are They? Carbonmade is the source for artists and designers of all sorts who want to build and manage online portfolios of all sorts — design, illustration, art, or any other creative work.

What They Do: Carbonmade solves a really basic problem: millions of creative people in the world need Web exposure but have neither the time nor the skills to do the nuts-and-bolts work of putting together an online "showplace."

Enter Carbonmade — enabling them to spend their creative "juice" on their art, and not on fussing with portfolios! [118] And Carbonmade does this for lots and lots and LOTS of people: at last count, some 400,000 designers — including free account users.[119] But even upgrading to a "premium" account won't deflate your wallet: for a mere $12 per month, you can upload and manage 50 projects, 500 images, and 10 videos...and more.

Where They Came From: 'Twas a bleak December day in 2005, and Dave Gorum (@davegorum) had a headache. No, not from a winter flu bug — but from the frustrating and, at times, costly efforts involved in putting his illustration work online.[119]

"This shouldn't be this hard," Dave complained to his programming buddy, Jason Nelson.
Technical guru and co-founder Jason Nelson (@iamcarbon) agreed. "And it doesn't have to be. Watch this." (Poof!)

Well, okay, maybe it didn't happen *exactly* that fast. (Jason had loaned out his magic wand elsewhere, and didn't have it back yet.) But the two (eventual) founders put their heads together over the span of a week during the Christmas

---

[118] http://thestartupfoundry.com/2011/05/24/why-carbonmade-decided-to-bootstrap-and-go-freemium/
[119] http://carbonmade.com/about

holidays; when they emerged from their brainstorming marathon, the first iteration of Carbonmade was born. [119]

Little did they know what they'd just created! Originally meant as a tool to make life easier for Dave his fellow designers, Carbonmade fast became a "secret" too good to keep. By 2007, the co-founders had their startup going so well that they could drop other client work and nurture the "new baby" full-time.[119] And a grand (and full) time has been had by all ever since!

You Design...They Do the Rest

Company: Campaign Monitor
Website: www.campaignmonitor.com
Last Known Revenue: > $1 Million[120]

Who They Are: Campaign Monitor is a company dedicated to making it easy for YOU to use email marketing software — if you're a designer who does marketing for your clients. Their slogan? "You design, we'll do the rest."

How They're Doing It: What is "the rest"? White-label rebranding of their services. This allows the designer to pay Campaign Monitor and then build that into the price they in turn pass on to their own clients. Prices range from $15 per month, for up to 500 customers, to $500 per month for half a million subscribers. Today more than 100,000 designers, agencies, and "amazing companies" of all shapes and sizes rely on Campaign Monitor to manage their email marketing. On any given week, they add more than 1,000 new customers to this list — and they've doubled revenues and profits every year for the last six years.[120]

Where They Came From: Campaign Monitor was the brainchild of founders Ben Richardson and David Greiner in their last year of college in 2004. Originally, the co-founders focused on Web design; the software idea, as does so much in the world of the entrepreneur, came out of frustration! They were designing email newsletters for a lot of their clients but couldn't find the right tool for the job. So, after they tried everything on the market, they "built the better mousetrap" — more accurately, a better app — themselves, one that let their clients manage their own newsletters. The clients loved it, and it became a nice new revenue stream. [120]

Then the question occurred to them: were there other Web designers who shared their pain? The answer, as it turned out, was a resounding YES...and they knew they were on to something.[121] Continuing to spend an hour or two every day tweaking the product, talking to the customers, and making improvements, they soon saw Campaign Monitor revenues catch up to their consulting business.

---

[120] http://37signals.com/svn/posts/2342-profitable-proud-campaign-monitor
[121] http://www.campaignmonitor.com/our-story/

What did the founders learn in building Campaign Monitor?[122]

1. You can succeed in building a product to meet your specific needs.
2. You don't have to please everyone — focus on the needs of your most passionate users.
3. You must identify the "need-to-have" features, set a launch date, and stick with it.

As David Greiner says, "I think one of the best ways a company can build a relationship with their customers is to help them get better at something." [120]

Making better connections — it's something entrepreneurs do as second nature. For Campaign Monitor, it's paying off in high-level satisfaction...AND profits!

---

[122] http://www.slideshare.net/webdirections/what-we-learned-building-campaign-monitor

Creating Email Campaigns So Easy; Even a Monkey Could Do It

Company: MailChimp
Website: www.mailchimp.com
Last Known Revenue: Estimated at $100 Million+[123]

What They Do: MailChimp streamlines marketing processes with ease. At the click of a button a company can create advertisements and email flyers in an easy to use platform. These marketing procedures are quick and simple and make it possible for you to get your information out to the masses with little to no effort on your part.

MailChimp makes it easy for any marketer or business owner to design appealing email templates for your target audience without the need to hire a programmer or designer.   The reason why MailChimp is so effective is that the prototype version offers a package which takes effect monthly and allows you to start up for free.

How'd they do it: Back in 2001 MailChimp came about because its founder, Ben Chestnut (@benchestnut), was frustrated and fed up with the way his newsletters were going out to his customers. Ben was also the founder/CEO of another company called Rocket Science Group and he had some working business knowledge and also understood the importance of being able to network through newsletters. He applied his knowledge and the rest was history!

In the early days of MailChimp they found their humble beginnings in creating simple e-mail campaigns for clients. The demand and the technology grew and inevitably the business shot up to astounding levels and making multiple aspects of marketing simple, creative, and user friendly. They found a niche in the free market by opening up their services to more than just paid members and offering a free simple marketing tool and then allowing for more customizable features with the paid product.[124]

By opening up their services they created a dynamic business model that hoisted their numbers to 450,000 members by 2010 and the

---

[123] http://www.quora.com/How-much-revenue-is-MailChimp-doing
[124] http://blog.mailchimp.com/going-freemium-one-year-later/

profit sky rocketed at over 650% in 12 months! In this hectic and every changing world they have managed to find their niche and offer their service without outside funding.[124]

The early trial and errors of the company have made them stronger and they rely heavily on client feedback and word of mouth. They're a pretty awesome company, so it seems that they'll keep movin' on up!

Oh! What we can do when we put our minds to work!

Hitting the Mark with SEO "Hustle"

Company: Slingshot SEO
Website: www.slingshotseo.com
Last Known Revenue: $10.9 Million (2012)[125]

Who They Are: Slingshot SEO is a search engine optimization consulting agency that leads companies to the top of search engine results and drives more traffic to their websites.

How They're Doing It: With a bang! They're an Inc.com 5000 company that has grown more than 3,000% over the past 3 years[125]—by concentrating on doing ONE thing spectacularly well. Today, Slingshot SEO remains one of the few agencies with an exclusive focus on enterprise SEO. For many, the allure of other services is just too great, but for Slingshot SEO, their focus is their competitive advantage. This focus enables them to meet the varied and changing needs of enterprise clients over significant stretches of time.

Where They Came From: Slingshot SEO was co-founded by Kevin Bailey, Aaron Aders (@aaronaders), and Jeremy Dearringer (@PapaSlingshot) in 2006. Starting with a pool of $10,000 as their first and only investment, they built the company by first taking on unprofitable projects to "show their chops."
The screamingly-tight budget also meant that none of them took a salary for the first year, instead putting every dollar they earned back into the company. They even cut a deal with their first customer: if their SEO services proved to be successful for their client, that client would in turn tell three other companies about their experience.

...and so on, and so on!

They didn't hit a home run right away, however; at first, they tried to be "all things Internet marketing." That proved to be too scattered a modus operandi for success. When they narrowed their niche to SEO only, however, they knew they "had" something—and could be more innovative than other companies in the SEO space.[126]

---

[125] http://www.inc.com/profile/slingshot-seo

That innovation springs not only from a singular focus but from the terms under which they started—technically, a "shoestring"! They had to develop a mindset of minimizing waste, uncovering the most efficient processes, and maximize every dollar they had. From this desire to be nimble and adaptable came the company's proprietary SEO workforce management software: it enables them to track workflow, valuable information upon which to increasingly streamline their operations.

When asked for a few words of wisdom, the owners were quick to respond:

"If you have dreams of building an Inc. 500 company on a bootstrap, believe that it can be done. You've just got to be flexible and focused, you've got to be innovative, and you've got to treat your customers right."[126] Or, as their website puts it: "Slingshot SEO exists because we *love* the Internet and are endlessly fascinated by the way it's changing the world and serving people."[127]

Changing the world + serving people = a great formula for aiming at business success. And with Slingshot SEO's "customer first" approach, a company can hit the "bull's eye" every time!

[126] http://www.inc.com/kevin-bailey/build-a-fast-growing-company-on-a-bootstrap-budget.html
[127] http://www.slingshotseo.com/about/

Launching a Company With Feedback From Your Clients

Company: SurveyGizmo
Website: www.surveygizmo.com
Last Known Revenue: $5.1 Million (2011)[128]

What They Do: SurveyGizmo is a dynamic site that allows you to create marketing surveys, questionnaires and forms. They offer comprehensive packages that vary from $49 - $150 a month depending on your need. So far they already boast 150,000 customers and have helped to create over 200 MILLION surveys for their customers! That's a lot of information gathered!

How'd They Do It: In 2006, two internet savvy techies from Boulder, Colorado thought up SurveyGizmo and created the company from the ground up. Christian Vanek (@CVanek) and Scott McDaniel (@scottmcdaniel) were co-workers at another internet based powerhouse (MarketingSherpa – another company that we highlight) and realized that the people weren't completely satisfied with survey software that was available to them.

The two men kept their project under wraps and while continuing to work their day jobs they created a new system to help people get the most out of their information gathering software. They used their own funds and capital and even picked up a few clients! It was actually because of their job with MarketingSherpa that they could talk to people and get instant feedback about what their needs were. They were literally in the marketing trenches of their future business.[128]

They started slow and like most startup companies, with a lot of trial and error. During the first few months they worked with a handful of customers on which features to build and listened intently to what was missing from their product and other similar ones on the market. Rather than paying for this start up feedback, SurveyGizmo offered their customers free lifetime use of their software.[129]

---

[128] http://www.dailycamera.com/business/ci_19835797

Since they came onto the scene in 2006 the company has been growing by leaps and bounds. In 2011 Christian Vanek was named one of Colorado's Top Young Professionals and the company has made a name for itself through word of mouth marketing[130] as well as catching the eyes of some bigger fish, so to speak.

Some of their customers are Fortune 500 companies, education institutions, and some heavy hitting non-profit organizations. By allowing their company to grow based on merit of the product alone they have already managed to double their staff and run over 200 million surveys![130] Pretty amazing stuff in such a short time!

[129] http://www.surveygizmo.com/survey-blog/surveygizmos-christian-vanek-among-top-5-of-colorados-top-25-young-professionals-for-2011-coloradobiz-magazine/
[130] http://www.prweb.com/releases/2012/1/prweb9094890.htm

A Father and Son Team Find a Profitable Niche in Digital Photos

Company: SmugMug
Website: www.smugmug.com
Last Known Revenue: $12 Million+[131]

What They Do: SmugMug is an online photo sharing website for amateur and professional photographers that is self-funded and has been profitable for over three years.[132]

SmugMug offers amateur and professional photographers features such as watermarking, ability to sell prints, and create online galleries of photos that help promote their work. Photographers can use their own domain names to connect with SmugMug which helps photographers build in social features making it easy for photographers and their fans to share their work.[132]

SmugMug charges its users between $40 - $150 per year. The more expensive packages provide photographers with e-commerce capabilities that enable them to sell their photographs directly from SmugMug. SmugMug of course handles and processes the orders, giving photographers the free time they need to focus on, well, their photography.

How'd They Do It: Founded in 2002 by Father and son duo, Chris (@baldy) (father) and Don MacAskill (@DonMacAskill) (son), SmugMug has grown into a $12 million-a-year operation with 100,000 subscribers and was profitable in the first year, after it reached 10,000 subscribers.[131]

Thriving in a competitive market, SmugMug has built a solid reputation among amateur and professional photographers for their impeccable service and strong ability to save photographers time from having to deal with the administrative work associated with promoting and selling their digital prints.

---

[131] http://www.usatoday.com/tech/products/2008-02-19-smugmug_N.htm
[132] http://www.crunchbase.com/company/smugmug

SmugMug benefits from a network effect as well. Once photographers see other photographers on the site, they become more attracted to it. The fear of being left out drives more and more photographers to sign up for the service. Building a sustainable business is of course more than just establishing a strong network effect, but SmugMug has found a way to keep its customers happy, while maintaining a profitable online business.

Father Chris initially ponied up $200,000 to get SmugMug up and off the ground and to later fuel their fast growth and to expand their team, added an additional $300,000 to the company. The father/son duo got to within $50,000 of running through the entire $500,000[133] they put into their startup before they hit positive cash flow during their first year of operations.[131]

Chris previously founded and sold the online bookstore, FatBrain, to Barnes & Noble for $60 million, providing him the opportunity to be the only investor in his son's venture. [131]

SmugMug initially started out as a gaming and social network site that also enabled users to share photos, but the founders saw a bigger opportunity in the photo-sharing business and doubled down by rebranding as SmugMug.[134]

So what's next for the father/son duo? Well according to Chris, SmugMug has turned down numerous buyout inquiries from companies, including one from Nokia.[134]

[133] http://mixergy.com/smugmug-chris-macaskill-interview/
[134] http://www.bizjournals.com/sanjose/stories/2008/08/04/smallb1.html?page=all

Take Your Time and Do Your Homework!

Company: Synthesio
Website: www.synthesio.com
Last Known Revenue: Undisclosed

Who They Are: Synthesio provides social media-monitoring services for leading global companies like McDonald's, Nike, Johnson & Johnson, Toyota, and more.

How They're Doing It: Synthesio has doubled sales three years running and was expected to do the same in 2011.[135]

Where They Came From: In 2006, a handful of people were thinking about the importance of monitoring social media for big brands as if their reputations depended on it—and thus, Synthesio was born. The co-founders, Loic Moisand (@LoicMo) and Thibault Hanin (@ThibaultHanin), are described as having two totally different profiles: one's in charge of product development, the other, sales and consulting. This "yin" and "yang" approach has helped ensure their products and services stay balanced between hi-tech and hi-touch. [135]

They bootstrapped the business based on the motto, "Money doesn't make you smart." But brainpower does—and in several distinct ways, Synthesio shows off the power of extra thought...and time. Although many aspects of social media move like the wind, Synthesio's founders had other ideas—like spending a full two years on product development. [135]

"We really worked slowly," explained Moisand, who personally conducted research among 400 professionals in order "to really understand how social media could help them on a daily basis." When they finally launched their monitoring tool in 2008, the market was just about ready for it. [135]

Of course, so was competition; however, once more, the founders' unique approach paid off. In the world of software as a service, the "service" part of the equation is often almost an afterthought. Synthesio, on the other hand, added consulting services on top of its initial monitoring platform after about a year, a decision that

---

[135] http://www.fastcompany.com/1731059/7-oh-so-easy-steps-doubling-your-sales

once again set them apart from competitors such as Radian 6. Armed with a team of analysts and consultants, Synthesio has the wherewithal to truly help their clients navigate through the ever-changing social landscape. [135]

One of Synthesio's core beliefs is that startups need to hold onto their customers as best they can. This approach to their business has given the company a 90% client retention rate and numerous industry accolades and awards. Moisand explains, "We really want to nurture our clients and help them understand what they can do with their online reputation.[135]

In the end, just as it was with the initial questions in 2006, it's all about reputation. Moisand and Hanin know their clients' good names and degrees of success really *do* depend on keeping their social media reputations sterling. In turn, operating with that aim front-and-center has made Synthesio shine as well!

Company: Context Optional
Website: www.contextoptional.com
Last Known Revenue: Estimated at $10 Million+

Who They Are: Context Optional is a "dashboard" that provides marketers with comprehensive solutions to build, manage, monitor, and measure brand presence across social networks. They've made quite the name for themselves by building a social media platform that enabled Fortune 2000 brands to create, monitor, and measure social marketing success.

How They're Doing It: With the Social Marketing Suite, a powerful and integrated enterprise social marketing platform that is built to scale with needs, capable of supporting large numbers of pages and enterprise administrators and tens of millions of fans.[136] It delivers effective social Customer Relationship Management (CRM) and marketing solutions— things like coupons and quizzes — that "blow the (proverbial) doors" off the results of standard Facebook entries.[136]

Where They Came From: Context Optional was founded in 2006 by Scott Kleper (@klep) and Kevin Barenblat (@barenblat), and its genius entailed cashing in on burgeoning social media by being in the right place, at the right time, with the right product. In Scott's own words: "When we started Context Optional, we accurately predicted the rise of Facebook as a viable marketing platform down to almost every detail."[137]

This wasn't the first time Kleper and Barenblat were visionary, either. They'd already proven themselves pretty good at customizing apps even before Context Optional, when they co-founded SpotDJ, a social music application that lets the user "be the DJ." (Fess up. Everyone wants to do that at one time or another, right?)

---

[136] http://socialtimes.com/context-optional-streamlines-enterprise-facebook-engagement_b17976
[137] http://www.contextoptional.com/blog/2011/05/

Predicting what people want to be able to control, measure, enjoy and profit from — and giving them the means to do it — has made their "vision" pay off big: Context Optional was acquired for a reported $50 Million in May 2011 by Adobe Efficient Frontier.[138] What "frontiers" these two may conquer next might not even be on the "drawing boards" yet...but they'll no doubt be on the cutting edge when those new visions become reality.

---

[138] http://www.allfacebook.com/efficient-frontier-acquires-context-optional-2011-05

Online Gaming

"There are some who want to change the channel;
there are others that want to change the world."
~unknown

The Social Game Developer That Sold For $35M

Company: KlickNation
Website: www.klicknation.com
Last Known Revenue: Undisclosed

What They Do: KlickNation is a social game developer that has created Facebook game hits such as *Superhero City* and *Age of Champions*. Using what's called a freemium business model to generate sales, KlickNation offers its games for free, but charges users to purchase superpowers, weapons, and other in-game assets that enhance the gamers experience and ability to reach new levels.

How They're Doing It: Mark Otero went from business school (at my alma mater – UC Davis Graduated School of Management) to frozen yogurt store-owner, to the founder of KlickNation. He eventually sold this company for $35 Million. Mark founded KlickNation in 2006 after quitting his corporate job at Franklin Templeton. He cashed out the $75,000 in his 401k. He *knew* it wasn't going to be enough to get a gaming company off the ground, so instead, Mark opted to open Mochii – a frozen yogurt shop in Sacramento. It would serve as a cash vehicle to fund his gaming company on the side.[139]

By day, Mark ran the frozen yogurt shop, but by night, he transformed into the manager of a team of developers helping develop the first social games that he would eventually sell.

At one point, Mark ran up several hundred thousand dollars of tax and credit card debt, and his back was literally up against the wall. Running short of cash and time, the KlickNation team launched *Clash of Heroes* and *Superhero City* on Facebook. Mark and KlickNation started out earning a mere $50 a day in game sales, but thanks in part to the games' popularity; they quickly grew to $1,000 a day in revenues. Within a month, KlickNation was bringing in $5,000 a day - they would never look back. [139]

---

[139] Sactown Magazine – Feb/Mar 2012.

KlickNation continued to develop popular social games under this freemium model, and with its success, KlickNation went on to launch several other social games that brought in millions of dollars in revenue before eventually selling it to multi-*billion* dollar company, EA.[140] Game – Set – Match!

Banking on the world's love of entertainment, not to mention their penchant for upgrades and increased power, Mark and his team turned a mere glimmer of an idea into a blinding success!

Otero's success has been news worthy of late, as it has been reported he is buying a minority stake in the NBA franchise, Sacramento Kings.[141]

This is a formula for success – and you can take *that* to the bank as well!

---

[140] http://www.insidesocialgames.com/2011/12/30/2011s-social-game-related-mergers-acquisitions-inside-social-games-and-appdatas-performance-review/
[141] http://www.cowbellkingdom.com/2013/01/22/kevin-johnson-introduces-sacramento-based-buyers-in-effort-to-save-the-kings/

Company: Storm8
Website: www.storm8.com
Last Known Revenue: Estimated at $50 Million[142]

What They Do: Known to be the most true-to-form game creators, Storm8 promises to earn the role they have received as the creators of the most well used and enjoyed role playing game, World War, compatible with the iPhone, iPod Touch as well as the ever famous Android Device. Storm 8 has become the "largest mobile social games developer in the U.S.", and Storm8's studio, TeamLava, has been recognized as THE #1 Mobile Social Game Developer.[143]

The team at Storm8 has managed to continually put out impressive games which won them a place in the Top 10 best App providers with more than 210 million downloads, 5 billion play sessions and 18 billion minutes of games played. As a result they have significantly large and continuous revenue utilized in game which creates real money for the creators.

How'd They Do It: Perry Tam and Garret Remeshe were former employees of the Mighty Facebook and after leaving the company made it possible for them to found Storm8 in 2009 and it's only been up from there!

Using the networking skills developed while working with Facebook, Storm 8 continues to clear its own road on the market and as of 2012, this company, significantly made up of ex Facebook Employees, has reached upwards of 50 employees and is growing strong.[144] Take that Mark Zuckerburg!

Storm8 continues to grow and so far has never had to raise money or become funded by any kind of corporate expenditure for any reason. The employees who are chosen to work for Storm8 are excellent with graphics, providing an excellent marketing style with a good game engine. They

---

[142] http://www.insidemobileapps.com/2011/06/08/storm8-perry-tam-1-million/
[143] http://techcrunch.com/201106/22/a-new-mobile-social-games-king-in-the-u-s-former-facebookers-take-storm8-to-210-million-downloads/

have a great model to continue their growth because they only hire the best in order to give the best product.

"We understand our users well and adapt our games for them," Tam said. "We also introduce our games at a rapid pace, or about one a month."[144]

---

[144] http://venturebeat.com/2011/07/08/storm8-comes-on-strong-with-three-new-android-games-exclusive/

Events

"The day your past is more exciting than your future, you have stopped living."

~ John Wooden

Kissing a "Frog" Has Never Been Profitable Before!

Company: Red Frog Events
Website: www.redfrogevents.com
Last Known Revenue: $50 Million (2011)[145]

Who They Are: Red Frog Events is the name for a fun bunch—the people who are behind such things as Warrior Dash, Great Urban Race, Red Frog Bar Crawls, and Beach Palooza. (With event names like that, you know the people behind them have "fun" as a required personality trait.) The U.S. Chamber of Commerce apparently thinks they're fun, too: Red Frog Events won their 2011 DREAM BIG Small Business of the Year Award.[146]

How They're Doing It: As they put it, "laughing all the way"—with style, panache, and some impressive numbers. Since its humble beginning, Great Urban Race has grown to over 35 events in 2011 with many races having over 500 participants.[145]

Where They Came From: Inspiration—courtesy of an episode of *The Amazing Race*. Joe Reynolds (@redfrogevents), the company founder, saw that show and started thinking, "Hmmm. We ought to do a Chicago version of this." The idea took hold and wouldn't let go; with $5,000 in savings, he put together a "pilot" version of his own, the first Great Urban Race, in September of 2007—and drew 156 people. When he saw that, Reynolds says, he knew he had a viable business.[147]

Of course, from the start, he also had people telling him that his business idea was no good! [148] Once again, though, his inspiration and resourcefulness proved them wrong: with a very small budget to host their first Great Urban Race, Joe enlisted local business "partners" to help offset event costs. In exchange, those local businesses got great exposure, and Joe was even able to turn a profit.

---

[145] http://www.inc.com/guides/201107/how-to-profit-from-a-passion-for-sports.html
[146] http://www.freeenterprise.com/article/small-businesses-make-a-big-difference-0
[147] http://articles.chicagotribune.com/2011-06-19/business/ct-biz-0619-confidential-races-20110619_1_staycation-ambition-craze
[148] http://blogs.ilstu.edu/business-magazine/2011/09/red-frog-events/

After finding success with Great Urban Race, the team and Joe launched Warrior Dash as their second event. Warrior Dash is a 5K obstacle race that challenges racers through fire, mud and barbed wire.

One of Warrior Dash's greatest innovations was how the company adapted the wave system to accommodate the highest number of participants in two days of races. Participants run every half hour in waves of 500 to 800 people. Due to its popularity, Warrior Dash has jumped from one race to 35 races in just two years with over 700,000 participants in 2011.[149]

Red Frog grew slowly, grossing a modest $50,000 its first year—but it soon "leapt" upward in scope and success. Its gross income for 2011 was expected to top $50 million.[150]

[149] http://www.stevieawards.com/pubs/awards/403_2649_21125.cfm
[150] http://www.inc.com/guides/201107/how-to-profit-from-a-passion-for-sports.html

Racing for Adventure, Fun, and (Lots of) Profit

Company: Tough Mudder
Website: www.toughmudder.com
Last Known Revenue: $70 Million[155]

Who They Are: Tough Mudder is an adventure sports company that hosts 10-to-12-mile endurance obstacle courses designed by British Special Forces to test all-around strength, stamina, mental grit, and camaraderie. Tough Mudder folks want you to stretch yourself and have a great time doing it!

How They're Doing It: The first-ever Tough Mudder event was held in May 2010, at Bear Creek ski resort in Pennsylvania. It attracted 4,500 participants and sold out in just 35 days.[151] And the hits just keep on comin': by the end of 2012, more than 500,000 participants are expected to have participated in and experienced a Tough Mudder event. That kind of success draws kudos, among them a semi-final ranking in Harvard's annual business plan competition.[152]

With Tough Mudder planning 30 events worldwide in 2012, and with an "admission charge" of $150 and up per participant, it's no wonder revenues are sky rocketing. Tough Mudder also secured corporate underwriting from such "names" as Under Armour, Bic, and Dos Equis. (The two-year Under Armour deal alone was worth an estimated $2-$3 million!)[153]

Where They Came From: Harvard MBA grad Will Dean was frustrated with the monotony of marathons and triathlons and was convinced there must be something better. As it turns out, there was—and working for British government counter-terrorism units showed him what that could be. After that first breakout event, Will put word-of-mouth and

---

[151] http://en.wikipedia.org/wiki/Tough_Mudder
[152] http://www.nytimes.com/2010/04/29/sports/29mudder.html?pagewanted=all
[153] http://www.forbes.com/sites/mikeozanian/2011/12/08/under-armour-signs-groundbreaking-deal-with-tough-mudder/

Facebook to work spreading the good news about Tough Mudder...and the rest, as the saying goes, is history.

It also didn't hurt that Will had his own successful history with previous ventures. Prior to Tough Mudder, he had founded two other companies: BollywoodOriginals.com, a vintage Bollywood poster online gallery, and Just William T-Shirts, which is a national supplier of UK university graduation tees. [154]

The combination of Will's entrepreneurial background, past work with the counter-terrorism unit, and formal business training from Harvard has made for a magical combination—and $70 million growth for Tough Mudder in less than two years.[155]

---

[154] http://toughmudder.com/press-room/founders-bio/
[155] http://www.inc.com/tim-donnelly/tough-mudder-conquering-obstacles-to-build-70-million-business.html

Being "Driven" Beyond a Six-Figure Salary

Company: Entrepreneur Week
Website: www.entrepreneurweek.net
Last Known Revenue: Undisclosed

Who They Are: Entrepreneur Week is people who host worldwide events for aspiring and current entrepreneurs—the perfect opportunity to meet your potential next business partner and rub elbows with those already "in the trenches."

How They're Doing It: Entrepreneur Week started modestly, as such enterprises go; from a "small idea with a big vision," they put together an initial event with 40 speakers and 600 attendees. Now, they host events with hundreds of speakers and thousands of entrepreneur attendees all over America. And, as if that's not enough, they've also launched globally—to the tune of some 25 cities around the world.

Where They Came From: Founder and UCONN grad, Gary Whitehill, passed on a six-figure salary—at the lowest dip of the recession!— to start Entrepreneur Week.[156] He explains:

"As a digital media and events company, we had a simple thesis: the economic downturn created opportunities for early-stage entrepreneurs, resulting in a need for actionable, high quality and relevant content—panels, keynotes, roundtables, mentoring sessions, educational resources and networking events—from a trustworthy forum."[157]

Sounds like a great idea, doesn't it? Whitehill thought it was a "bull's eye"—until he realized they had neglected to account for the lack of access to capital to scale the vision. He recalls that he "had the talent, timing, and value proposition, but it still wasn't enough— as far as investors were concerned."
So he did what any enterprising entrepreneur does: he bootstrapped the endeavor with $350,000 to mitigate the variable marketing and infrastructure costs. Entrepreneur Week's founders also adopted three startup strategies:[157]

---

[156] http://www.businessinsider.com/from-six-figure-salary-to-bootstrapped-startup-entrepreneur-week-2012-1
[157] http://theyec.org/from-six-figure-salary-to-bootstrapped-startup-entrepreneur-week/

- They went without salaries for the first year. Whitehill explains, "If money was an issue for any of us, [we decided] we'd loan it to one another in the short-term or beg our family and friends. We were all fairly young with no families or mortgage payments to worry about." That decision saved Entrepreneur Week roughly $160,000.[157]
- They created leverage in the marketplace by putting together a 90-day multifaceted networking plan to create in-kind donations of PR and marketing materials, printing, Web design, event spaces, and more. This strategy saved Entrepreneur Week over $200,000 in its first year. [157]
- They went virtual for a year, which meant the 15-person team worked remotely. Whitehill housed interns on living room couches and managers in spare bedrooms, and held strategy sessions every week—on the patio. "It was insane," he recalls, "but a strong team commitment made all the difference, and we saved roughly $65,000 that first year without expenses such as office space, heating, computers, desks, etc." [157]

His advice to other entrepreneurs? Do likewise: think outside the box, cut costs...and you, too, can grow your "small ideas" into "big visions" much faster than you might imagine. [157]

Cocktails and Entrepreneurs? Sign Me Up!

Company: Tech Cocktail
Website: www.tech.co
Last Known Revenue: Six figures[158]

Who They Are: Tech Cocktail is a media and events organization for startups, entrepreneurs, and technology enthusiasts. Their goal is simple: to amplify local tech communities and give entrepreneurs a place to get informed, connected, and inspired.

How They're Doing It: Tech Cocktail dedicates itself to covering news, how-tos, up-and-coming startups, industry trends online, and hosting entrepreneurial meet-up events in over 20 cities in the US and abroad. It earns money from direct ticket sales to the events, corporate sponsorships, and online advertising. Today, it is hosted in 20+ cities and has become such a huge hit that even prominent investors like Brad Feld (@bfeld) have started showing up to the networking events. [158]

Where They Came From: Frank Gruber (@frankgruber) and Eric Olson (@ericolson) founded Tech Cocktail to scratch their own "itch" to meet and network with local entrepreneurs. What better way to bring entrepreneurs together than to let some local startups showcase and present their companies? So, after he made a few connections through his job at the Tribune Company, Gruber got the idea to host a local event in his home city of Chicago—but decided to add a twist. In his eyes, the most comfortable type of networking could be done over cocktails...hence the name of the new venture![158]

The enterprise had a modest start: the first event netted 250 attendees who heard about it after a lot of hustle, leveraging Eric's blog community, and local word-of-mouth. But there was one small problem: they weren't able to get a liquor license in time! Nevertheless, the efforts met with early enthusiasm, and the part-time "labor of love" soon turned into local events in four cities, with 1,000+ fans in attendance. [158]

This success with Tech Cocktail and the rich opportunity that lay in front of him made Gruber want to give this a go full-time. However,

---

[158] http://mixergy.com/frank-gruber-tech-cocktail-interview/

this meant bucking competition that had already sprung up, grabbing for portions of his market—and it meant giving up his cushy corporate job at AOL. With two- to three-months' salary in hand as part of his exit package from AOL, Frank reached out to a buddy—Eric Olson, who at the time was planning his wedding and in the midst of his MBA program at University of Chicago. Was Olson up for a full-time entrepreneurial gig? At that point, the answer was no; Eric decided to focus on his other priorities and declined to join Frank on a full-time basis. [158]

Gruber persevered, however, with excellent results. After seeing the success of their conferences take off, he and his team built out a wildly successful online media site, offering entrepreneurs even more of a resource to learn from each other. [158]

So how much money is there in events? According to Tech Cocktail, corporate sponsorship range from $500 to $5,000—although some sponsors will purchase multiple sponsorships, netting Tech Cocktail up to $25,000 from one sponsor at a single event. The difference? $500 gets you a logo placement, while $5,000 can earn you a title sponsorship of the event.

What's Gruber's perspective on getting a startup so successfully "started"?

"It takes a long frickin' time to build a business," he says. "I mean, I know a lot of people want to have the quick win and get their funding and grow to a bazillion people, and it's going to be a parade down the street... and that's not what's going to happen, necessarily. Especially if you're bootstrapped and you're doing something that's unique. I don't know anybody else that's crazy enough to go to twenty cities last year and host events everywhere—you know what I mean?" [158]

We think we do. And the eager networkers who show up for a little "tech" and a few "cocktails" certainly do. They're hoping the "craziness" continues for a long time.

Education

"First they ignore you. Then they laugh at you. Then they fight you. Then you win." ~Ghandi

Company: Revolution Prep
Website: www.revolutionprep.com
Last Known Revenue: $18.8m[159]

Who They Are: Revolution Prep is a group of some very smart students and alumni from some of the best universities in the U.S., gathered together to help students facing many varieties of those dreaded standardized exams that mean so much in the college-acceptance game (SAT and ACT in particular).

How They're Doing It: Through varied means, including group classes, private tutoring, and online courses. Building on the success of their initial SAT program, they now address a wide range of academic areas besides the SAT and ACT—among them the GRE (Graduate Record Exam) and high-stakes No Child Left Behind testing—and also feature a program that offers scholarships to students who otherwise could not afford their services.

Where They Came From: The company was formed in 2002, when founders Ramit Varma and Jake Neuberg met at UCLA's Anderson School of Business. Ramit and Jake had a passion for education—they had already taught for two of the biggest educational names in the business, Kaplan and the Princeton Review. But, as most innovators do, after a while, they thought, "We can do this even better." They immediately set to work proving just that: fine-tuning traditional educational tools and creating new and innovative solutions to academic problems, they created their own SAT "Reasoning Test" curriculum...and knew they were onto something.[159]

Others took note, too. By the spring of 2010, Revolution Prep was collaborating with the Partnership for LA Schools to offer free SAT classes to students at the Santee Educational Complex in Los Angeles. The results? Astonishing, to say the least. Students in the class improved up to *240 points* on their SAT exam scores, and Revolution

---

[159] http://www.inc.com/inc5000/profile/revolution-prep

Prep was commended in an open letter by Los Angeles Mayor Antonio Villaraigosa. [159]

And the hits just keep on comin'! In June 2010, Revolution Prep acquired test prep and admissions consulting company Ivy Insiders, enabling to offer tutoring specifically from Ivy League alums. This Santa Monica, CA, company has subsequently been named the fastest growing educational company in Los Angeles, not to mention ranking fourteenth fastest-growing in education nationwide, as listed in the 2010 *Inc.* 5000.[160]

Helping students learn—and test—better: an idea that's "revolutionary" in all the right ways!

---

[160] http://en.wikipedia.org/wiki/Revolution_Prep

The Social Network For Future MBAs

Company Name: Beat the GMAT
Website: www.beatthegmat.com
Last Known Revenue: $ 700,000 - $1 Million[161] (2012)

What They Do: Beat the GMAT is the world's largest social network for MBA applicants, serving over 2 million people each year. They are currently one of the leading online communities for pre-MBAs to learn everything they want (or need) to learn about applying to and attending business school.

Beat the GMAT earns affiliate revenues for sending prospective student to GMAT test preparation companies like Kaplan, and currently has 4 employees.

How They're Doing It: Eric Bahn created Beat the GMAT in the spring of 2005 from his Stanford University dorm room. As a Sociology grad student, Eric became quite interested in social networking theory and decided to put his education to a real world test by creating a social network to help pre-MBAs crack the confounded GMAT.

According to Eric, he has only put a whopping $4 (*four dollars!*) into the business – and that was just to buy the domain. The rest was simply an investment of his time to build and promote the website.[161]

Do you have to go to business school to start Beat the GMAT? No, Eric never went to business school. He *did* take the GMAT, however, and scored an impressive 720 (out of a possible 800).[162]

What does this teach us? First and foremost, it teaches that having a cash cow or two in your back yard isn't always a prerequisite. Secondly, it proves that with an idea, a vision, a passion for something, your time, and that old familiar word; determination – it truly can pay off.

---

[161] http://techcrunch.com/2011/07/20/beat-the-gmat-mba-watch/
[162] http://www.beatthegmat.com/mba/beat-the-gmat-team/eric-bahn

Time can often be *gold*, and Eric has proven that it can have huge benefits.

What's the best part? Well, no matter how much of it you spend, you'll always have more waiting right behind it!

Return-On-Investment doesn't always have to mean invested *money*.

Eric is a prime example that investments come in all shapes and sizes – and are relative.

In October, 2012, Beat the GMAT was acquired by Hobson's for an undisclosed sum.[163]

---

[163] http://www.bizjournals.com/cincinnati/news/2012/10/23/hobsons-acquires-beat-the-gmat.html

David Takes on Goliath in the Test Prep Industry

Company: Veritas Prep
Website: www.veritasprep.com
Last Known Revenue: $10 Million (2008)

What They Do: Veritas Prep provides GMAT test preparation and admissions consulting for pre-MBA, Law, and Medial School students. They offer live GMAT prep courses in more than 90 cities worldwide, as well as interactive online courses. Additionally, Veritas Prep offers admissions consulting services for applicants seeking admission to the most competitive business, law, and medical schools in the world.

Admission consulting is tailored to the schools that students are planning on applying to. Veritas Prep charges students $3,700 for admission consulting to a single school, and up to $11,400 for consulting on applying to 8 different schools. Hourly admission consulting is also available, at a rate of $750. Veritas Prep offers a highly tailored and customized consulting service by helping prospective students with every aspect of the admissions process (e.g., admissions letter, interview prep, resume-writing, and more).

Entrepreneur Magazine named founders, Markus Moberg and Chad Troutwine, two of its Trailblazers and Trendsetters of 2009.[164]

How They're Doing It: Founded in 2002 by graduates Markus Moberg and Chad Troutwine (@ChadTroutwine) of the Yale School of Management, Veritas Prep started off as a project for an entrepreneurship class where they earned 3rd place in the annual business plan competition. These co-founders used the $20,000 from that competition to launch Veritas Prep full-time.[165]

Industry leaders such as Kaplan have dominated the test prep industry, but by focusing exclusively on *graduate*

---

[164] http://www.veritasprep.com/blog/2010/01/veritas-prep-co-founders-named-two-of-entrepreneur-magazines-trailblazers-and-trendsetters-of-2009/
[165] http://www.entrepreneur.com/article/200014

schools, Veritas Prep carved out a specific niche catering to the hundreds of thousands of students that apply to business, law, and medical schools each year.

Markus and Chad took their knowledge and experience in applying to and attending a top business school, and successfully leveraged it to develop a program that meets the needs of students everywhere seeking to take the GMAT test and apply to competitive business schools.

Another exemplary example of a couple of well-schooled and academically successful guys using their ingenuity, knowledge and determination, to find a carved-out niche that was underrepresented in the world.

They saw the need, they knew the solution – and seized it with both hands!

That, my friends, is how you succeed in business!

Bringing Code Writing and Programming into a Whole New "League"!

Company: The Starter League
Website: www.starterleague.com
Last Known Revenue: $1 Million (2012)[168]

Who They Are: Neal Sales-Griffin (@nealsales) and Mike McGee (@michaelmcgee) are "the artists formerly known as Code Academy," and they offer classroom-based computer programming classes in the greater Chicago area. But they do more than that. They want to be "a group of passionate and persistent people that care deeply about adding value to the world through design, product, and business skills, in addition to coding. Just as we have with coding, we're here to prove that these skills are not limited to a chosen few, but can be learned by anyone who is driven by a problem they want to solve, regardless of their background." [166]

How They're Doing It: Now in their third season, they offer a wide range of classes, support, and mentorship. As the founders put it, "We see ourselves as the accelerator before the accelerator."

Where They Came From: Northwestern alumni Sales-Griffin, a business major, and McGee, a graphic design and political science major, knew nothing about software development when they decided to take twelve months and learn code themselves. So they looked for help: Web sites, classes, materials, and any other resources they could find.

"We really wanted to respect and learn the process [of coding]," said McGee. "So we did that and it was awesome, but it was pretty frustrating at times when you're stuck trying to learn, and you have no one to turn to, to get help. We spent a year [trying to learn how to code] and it shouldn't have took this long to get to where we were. So we decided to create an environment where it's fun to learn, you're learning around other passionate people, you get taught by a professional instructor, and you have mentors who are professional software developers." [167]

---

[166] http://www.starterleague.com/tar/posts/introducing-the-starter-league
[167] http://www.blackenterprise.com/technology/code-academy-teaches-web-development-to-the-masses/

That's how Code Academy was born, with a simple initial concept: 12 students each would pay $6,000 to learn how to code in 12 weeks, 12 hours each week. So, once they visionary duo learned enough to toss together a functional site that would help them drum up some capital to get their idea off the ground, the two quit their jobs and spent the summer of 2011 meeting and pitching investors.

Of course, they found a bunch of support along the way, but no capital. "Every time we met with somebody, we were one more email, one more meeting away from getting funded. But that next email or meeting never happened," recalls McGee.[168]

So the next question became how could they make the startup happen anyway? After all of their promising leads fell through, they decided to bootstrap the startup with tuition from their users—and that's where things got interesting!

The founders wanted 12 students for that first semester, but ended up with over 80 applications from people from various industries and backgrounds. They interviewed over 40 applicants and accepted 35 students. "Meeting those people, who we knew were out there...was the best week of my life," McGee says.

From those connections, the concepts—and the business—have mushroomed. They were presented with an opportunity to rent space in Groupon's headquarters, where they held their first classes. They found their first instructor, Jeff Cohen, through the Twitterverse. Similarly, a meeting with Steve Collens, senior vice president of Chicago's Pritzker Group and its investment arm, New World Ventures, landed them as the first tenants in a brand-spanking-new facility called 1871 (after the year of the Chicago Fire), a technology-oriented startup hub in the famed Merchandise Mart .[169]

Although still on the "ground floor" of their own startup, they've already received requests to emulate this model all over Chicago, not to mention the rest of the U.S. And these "starters" are ready to take up the baton: future plans include reaching out to youth, the economically disadvantaged, and minorities to provide coding, development, and design opportunities.

---

[168] http://mixergy.com/neal-sales-griffin-starter-league-interview/
[169] http://www.builtinchicago.org/blog/starter-league-founders-giving-back-young-entrepreneurs-chicago-conference

That's only the beginning—the "start," if you will—for these two and their Code Academy/Starter League dream. As their blog puts it so eloquently, "We are not simply an academy for coders. We are a League of Starters."[170]

Looks like they've "started" something stupendous, indeed!

---

[170] http://37signals.com/svn/posts/3241-37signals-invests-in-the-starter-league

Getting "Wise"...and Getting Rich!

Company: WyzAnt
Website: www.wyzant.com
Last Known Revenue: >$10 Million (2012) [171]

Who They Are: In a word, teachers—lots of them! WyzAnt is the leading tutoring marketplace on the Web, with 63,000+ tutors offering private lessons in hundreds of subjects like math, science, test prep, foreign languages, music, computers, and much more.

How They're Doing It: WyzAnt earns its money from commissions, plain and simple. If a tutor books a lesson through the site, WyzAnt makes a share of the fee.

Where They Came From: It all started in the Ivy League, when Andrew Geant and Michael Weishuhn met on the track team as undergraduates at Princeton University. Once Geant graduated, however, he found himself underwhelmed by the prospect of following his friends to work on Wall Street—so he turned to math tutoring. That's when he had a light bulb moment: figuring out how and where to promote his services online. Turns out there was "no 'there' there." He realized he needed to put a solution in place for that dilemma...and WyzAnt was born. Knowing his buddy Weishuhn had the technical expertise to build the platform, he wasted no time renewing old college ties!

The initial money for their startup came from various sources: Geant's math tutoring funds, Wieshuhn's full-time software gig, and—of course—friends and family, who later contributed $10,000.

With limited seed money, the Bootstrappers bypassed more expensive domain names containing some variation of "tutor" in them. Instead, they devised "WyzAnt.com"... a clever pun not only on the word "wise" but on the founders' name as well.[172]

WyzAnt launched exclusively in Washington D.C., to test their model. At first, they recruited tutors by plastering local college campuses with fliers saying, "We're Hiring." This attracted tutors to sign up with them, but getting parents and students to pay for a

---

[171] http://mixergy.com/andrew-geant-wyzant-interview/
[172] http://articles.chicagotribune.com/2012-04-14/business/ct-biz-0415-bootstrapping-20120414_1_chicago-entrepreneurs-venture-capital-startups

local tutor online proved to be an initial challenge. Nevertheless, they tweaked the model and kept at it, and soon fliers around D.C. promoting their online tutor network started to show results.[171]

By the half-year mark in its fledgling life, WyzAnt was making $3,000 per month, enough for Weishuhn to quit his "regular" job to focus on WyzAnt full-time. The founders modeled their success in D.C. to expand into larger markets—and proceeded to grow WyzAnt to a $4 million concern before hiring their first employee. [171] Talk about your "lean, mean, profitable machine"!

What advice do the founders have for aspiring entrepreneurs? When asked, Geant was quick to dispense solid wisdom:

"Let the data guide you. Source all of your marketing efforts, define different goals and conversions, track the quality of traffic/leads for various sources, optimize for the right keywords, and don't hesitate to change directions if the numbers don't make sense."[173]

He concludes further, "It's one of my biggest recommendations to someone starting a business. Whether it's yours or an investor's, don't pump a ton of money into an unproven business concept. Start small and learn from your mistakes."[173]

Building on a foundation of prudent domain name selection, careful testing, and trial-and-error course corrections has proven their venture to be "wise," indeed—and Weishuhn and Geant to be "WyzAnts" in their own right!

---

[173] http://shoestringventure.com/en/2010/07/02/wyzant-to-connect-with-local-private-tutors-from-a-shoestring-budget/

Food & Drink

"Every man dies, not every man lives." ~William Wallace

Company: The Fruit Guys
Website: www.fruitguys.com
Last Known Revenue: >$10 Million (2008)[174]

Who They Are: The FruitGuys are purveyors of fresh seasonal fruit from local farms to some 3,000 American businesses of various sizes, from small family-run concerns to major Fortune 500 corporations. They deliver to some pretty posh "addresses" in the nation: Red Bull, Virgin America, Yamaha, VMWare, and Wells Fargo, among other industry leaders.

How They're Doing It: The FruitGuys are considered a pioneer in this field—and, as a pioneer, are constantly being "flattered" by imitators who've sprung up trying to do what they do better. In barely ten years, what began as two people and an old Honda Civic filled with fruit is now worth millions and keeps a staff of over 40 people hopping.[175]

The company is a splendid example of both the benefits of new attention being paid to "workplace wellness" and the desire to support local and organic food initiatives. They "think globally and act locally" in concrete ways— whether by helping clients establish athletic clubs at the office, reaching out to low-income communities, or working with farmers to maintain sustainable businesses.[174]

Where They Came From: Chris Mittelstaedt (@theseedfeed) founded The FruitGuys when his contacts at dot-com companies complained that the combination of junk food and/or vending machine fare, plus long hours spent at their offices, was making them feel sluggish and gain weight. So Mittelstaedt thought about workplace food...and how he could change it. Farm-fresh produce was the clear answer. [174]

He started promoting these products within San Francisco, using a combination of cold-calling and...shall we say...unique marketing tools: at one point, he even made appearances in a banana suit on

---

[174] http://www.entrepreneur.com/article/196304#
[175] http://en.wikipedia.org/wiki/The_FruitGuys

city streets to distribute free fruit and promulgate healthy eating habits. [174]

Sounds like a promising start, especially in a funky, creative place like California. But it didn't last.
In one sweeping dot-com bust, Mittelstaedt lost so much clientele—and business-building momentum—that he basically had to go back and "reboot" from scratch after The FruitGuys found themselves with $50,000 of bad debt and Mittelstaedt himself with $100,000 of personal debt. But an important insight came out of that "crash." As he explains: "We were growing so fast at the time, and I wasn't paying attention to my dashboard or thinking macroeconomically." So, as part of the "reboot," he tweaked his business setup to include a tighter credit policy, more variable costs, and national expansion.[176]

Such "rebooting" and tweaking wasn't unfamiliar territory for Mittelstaedt; necessity's always been an important "FruitGuys" fuel. Once upon a time (well, okay, in 1998), he was pulling down a princely $9.50 an hour at a temp job—and then learned his wife was pregnant. Knowing that money wasn't going to go far toward bassinets, bottles, and diapers, he dug in: starting 18-hour days at midnight, lugging heavy crates of produce, and making deliveries personally. [174]   You might call it his own personal "workplace fitness" plan...but his "fruition" (pun intended) is everybody's healthy gain today!

[176] http://www.entrepreneur.com/article/196304#

From Basement Brewers to Leading Microbrew

Company: New Belgium Brewery
Website: www.newbelgium.com
Last Known Revenue $127 Million (2009)[177]

What They Do: New Belgium Brewery has become a household name for those happy beer drinkers who love the delicious flavor of Fat Tire, IPA Ranger as well as Snow Day.

New Belgium is located in Fort Collins, CO and has demanded the attention of the world at large because of their efficient business practices which include a large number of happy employees, as well as becoming the 3rd largest microbrewery in the United States, lagging behind only Sierra Nevada and Boston Beer Company. [178]

How'd They Do It: The history behind New Belgium Brewery is an inspirational tale of ingenuity on the part of Jeff Lebesch and his wife Kim Jordan in 1991. Their humble beginnings originated in the Lebesch's home garage where Jeff had an undeniable passion for creating new beer flavors.

With a strong following they acquired on the road after a very inspiring bicycle tour of Europe, the Belgian Style Beer which they tasted pushed itself into the heart of Jeff and Kim and they began to brew their own at home. When Jeff first began this project, he was a simple engineer who had purchased a homebrew system, and built it up from scratch just as a hobby. But by the time he perfected his very first batch of Belgian brew he was the envy of all of his friends and neighbors, and with the following they had developed they were able to have a lot of people who were willing to try out some new beer.[179]

The flavor of their beer was so good that they knew they would have to purchase a microbrewery of their very own

---

[177] http://www.inc.com/inc5000/profile/new-belgium-brewing
[178] http://www.huffingtonpost.com/2012/02/07/top-20-craft-breweries_n_1238076.html#slide=642205
[179] http://www.newbelgium.com/brewery/company.aspx

and so they took a second mortgage out of their house worth $60,000 to do it.[179]

They knew it would be a risk, but it was one they were not only willing to take, but felt that they had to, for the betterment of the beer drinking world. Their simple beginnings took them from store to store, peddling their new beer to try to stir up a taste for it and in their first year they produced 3,300 cases of 22 ounce bottles. Of the different kinds of beers they put out, Fat Tire was the one which was the most welcomed and its popularity has continued to grow stronger with every passing year.[180]

With the beer sales continually growing, Kim and Jeff left their day jobs and decided to focus on getting the name of New Belgium out there full time. By 2002, the company was able to move into a huge warehouse where they quickly started to get out their beer in Colorado and other cities.

Let's toast to their success!

---

[180] http://www.fundinguniverse.com/company-histories/new-belgium-brewing-company-inc-history/

Making Granola Cool (and Profitable)

Company: Bear Naked Granola
Website: www.bearnaked.com
Last Known Revenue $65 Million (2007)[181]

What They Do: Bear Naked is one of the most esteemed health food businesses in the health food industry. One of the best-selling products put to the market by Bear Naked is their very own Bear Naked Granola. This delicious and satisfying product is the answer to the prayers of many health food folks around the Nation. Bear Naked also paves the health food road with their very own cereals, cookies, and health food bars.

How'd They Do It: The founders of this company, Brendan Synnott and Kelly Flatley went to high school together which is how their friendship began. They started to realize at a young age, while making their own delicious, homemade granola, how important having healthy food on the market would be and it was through their collaborations which made it possible for them to begin their careers in Health Food in 2002 when Health Food started to take up key residence in the health conscious world.[182]

It wasn't easy for the pair to make their granola important on the market, but they managed to partner up with local supermarket, Stew Leonard's, after having some of their representatives have a taste of their delicious granola. It was because of the Granola's individual and unique flavor as well as its organic origins set it apart from anything else that was available on the market, and as a result they were swept into the industry to begin their entrepreneurial adventure. [182]

These two were well loved in their community, and many wanted to see them happy and really believed in the product as well so many grocery stores in their area decided to provide the granola to the general public. Their grass roots beginnings are an inspiration to millions because they started out so humbly.

---

[181] http://www.nytimes.com/2008/01/27/nyregion/nyregionspecial2/27granolact.html

After each investing $3,500 into the company, Brendan and Kelly went without an income for two years managing to survive by staying with their parents and charging $200,000 in credit. They both mixed up their granola recipe in Kelly's house where her parents enjoyed breakfast every day. The space was too small for long term usage and when sales began to pick up, the pair moved into an industrial kitchen where they began to entertain funding offers for their fast growing health brand.[182]

Staying true to their roots, the couple decided to continue on funding their Granola business themselves. This ended up being the smartest thing they could have done because eventually Kashi (Kellogg owned) offered an estimated $60 million to buy them out.[182]

Bear Naked is by far one of the forerunners in America's beautiful history of creating something out of nothing and succeeding. They developed a business ethic which allowed them to produce an excellent Granola for the masses with a lot of good, old fashioned hard work.

---

[182] http://money.cnn.com/2008/02/05/smbusiness/bear_naked.fsb/index2.htm

"Dogged" Determination Leads to Brewery Success!

Company: BrewDog
Website: www.brewdog.com
Last Known Revenue: $11 Million (2012)[183]

Who They Are: BrewDog is the UK's fastest- growing brewery.

How They're Doing It: In a word, cautiously. BrewDog is growing but needs to keep a sharp eye on its cash flow. The company pays for its raw materials—such as hops, malt, and bottles—when they are ordered, but then, as many businesses do, they have to wait 60 days for their distributors to pay them. In order to avoid what could be a perilous cash gap, then, BrewDog offers a 3 percent discount if cash is received in 10 days. Fortunately, these partners are in the minority—most of them must pay before BrewDog ships its product to them. Only distributors in Sweden and Norway, where such things are government-owned, do not have to pay prior to delivery. [183]

But another key to their growth is in their public. In 2009, BrewDog became the first company in Europe to sell its company's shares online to fans for $361 apiece, as a means to give customers ownership in the company. Over 1,500 customers invested—and the profitability has soared as a result!

Where They Came From: Bored with their "traditional" jobs—and with what they called "stuffy ales" that dominated the beer market—24-year-old founders James Watt (@brewdogjames) and Martin Dickie (@MartinDickie) decided (over a glass of beer, natch) to follow their passion of brewing beer. They set up an admittedly pretty scary "brewery" in Martin's garage and created the first batch of what has now become known the world-over as Punk IPA, which they sent to a local beer and whiskey journalist. He liked it so much he told them they should set up shop more formally.

---

[183] http://www.inc.com/inc-advisor/case-study-how-brewdog-bootstrapped-$11-million.html

So, in short order, they scored a building to lease, scraped together $78,000 in savings, combined it with a $47,000 bank loan, and went out and bought second-hand stainless steel. They started their adventure by brewing tiny batches, filling bottles by hand and selling beers themselves at local markets out of the back of their van.[183]

Watt says, "The first year involved living, eating, and sleeping at the brewery—a drafty warehouse on Fraserburgh's coastline. Martin and I often worked 20-hour shifts, both to stay afloat but also to stay warm."[183]

Even with all that scrimping, however, during the first six months, BrewDog could barely generate the sales it needed to pay interest on its bank loan. The problem? Their type of brew didn't go over well in northeast Scotland; they needed a wider and different market. Scandinavia beckoned, as did the U.S.[183] But how to reach them?

BrewDog had no budget for expensive—or even cheap!—advertising. That's where other beer aficionados in the blogosphere came in. Reaching out that way worked, especially in Sweden. [183] But then they had another problem: they'd become exporters...and they still needed cash flow help!

So, once again tapping the network of beer writers, they gathered a list of the most influential ones and sent them samples. For a little over $2,000, they created a humorous YouTube video that quickly racked up 250,000 page views. Reviews raved about them, the blogosphere was talking—and they could then go to international distributors and say, "The marketing's done. All you need to do is sell product." [183]

Which more and more distributors every day are happy to do!

These and other creative approaches—transforming their "weaknesses" into strengths and allowing their customers to help pay the bills—have turned BrewDog's robust, flavorful beers into "liquid gold" the world over. By March 2012, BrewDog's products were available in over 27 countries, and 65 percent of its $11 million in 2011 sales came from outside the U.K.[183] ...and there's nowhere to go but up for these "brewmasters of success." [183]

Travel

"The possibilities are endless and numerous...once we decide to act and not react." ~ George Bernard Shaw

Sustainable Global Adventure Travel Finds its Mark

Company name: G Adventures (formerly Gap Adventures)
Website: www.gadventures.com
Last Known Revenue: $160 Million (2011)[184]

What They Do: G Adventures is the leader in worldwide sustainable adventure tours. Covering all 7 continents, G Adventures offers more than 1,000 adventure travels for everything from hiking, biking, sailing and more, to more than 100,000 clients.

Tours typically start as low as $849 for a Thailand sailing experience, to as much as $4,499 for a 21-day trip through China, Mongolia and Russia.

How They're Doing It: In 1990, Bruce Poon Tip founded G Adventures. With little more than two credit cards and a raging fire of passion to change the way we travelled, Bruce set out to create G Adventures after he returned from a backpacking trip in Asia.

Bruce's profound advice to budding entrepreneurs is, "Do something you love and you'll never work a day in your life."[185]

For the entire first *decade* of his business, Bruce pushed forward with a high tolerance for risk, but saw it as more of a mere challenge – and he did so without as much as a *dime* of a loan! [185] He explains, "I was very aggressive in building the business. Fortunately, I have a very high tolerance for risk, but that doesn't work so well for the bankers." [185]

He took the proverbial bull by the horns and stared it down. He built his business with a fervor and determination that, still today, is often unequalled.

Bruce says: "It takes a level of focus, hard work and determination to take the ideas inside your head and present it to the world,"[185]

[184] http://www.gadventures.com/news-media/press-release/New_Online_Marketing_Manager/
[185] http://sprouter.com/blog/bridging-the-gap-between-bootstrapping-and-startup-success/

Bring the ideas out of *your* head and show them off! Believe in your vision and others will follow suit.

He took a seed and watered it until it grew into a veritable money tree. You can do it too.

Nothing whatsoever can stand in your way if you believe in it and want it bad enough! Bruce is living proof of that.

Consumer Goods

"Once you decide to work for yourself, you never go back to working for somebody else." ~Alan Sugar

From the Beaches of San Diego to $35 Million in Hand Bag Sales

Company: Rebecca Minkoff LLC
Website: www.rebeccaminkoff.com
Last Known Revenue $35 Million (2011)[186]

What They Do: Rebecca Minkoff is a known brand which deals in a wide variety of luxury handbags, accessories and apparel which are designed with fun and interesting designs, making the product accessible to the general public.

How'd They Do It: Rebecca Minkoff first touched down on success through her original apparel company. She trusted her brother with his insight and made him the CEO of her company and together they managed to push the company global and by 2009 Rebecca was being honored as a New York Moves Power Woman because of her ability to thrive in adversity and get her product out.

Many of her products have the quirky power that tends to work out well when trending throughout larger city areas. Celebrities could be found wearing her 'I Love New York,' t-shirts. When she moved from t-shirts to handbags the market really took off.[186]

When it comes to creating a successful business, Rebecca Minkoff has several bits of advice to offer. She recommends the importance of always staying true to your individualistic desires of what you want your company to be like.

Don't get caught up in what others say that you have to do, the key to standing out is to be yourself. She also mentions that it is important for a person starting a business to know how much money you are going to want to spend in the long run, and make sure to price your products so that they are available to different kinds of buyers as well as allow for customers to provide feedback so that you know what it is that they want. [186]

186
http://online.wsj.com/article/SB10001424052970204059804577224990715958640.html?mod=WSJ_hps_sections_smallbusiness

The business took a bit of a hit when the recession began, but she managed to push on through and increased sales are expected to reach upwards of $55 million by 2012. [186]

A Booming Business Growing Too Fast For the Shark Tank

Company: OrigAudio
Website: www.origaudio.com
Last Known Revenue $5 Million (2012)[187]

What They Do: OrigAudio (a play on the word "Origami") manufactures eco-friendly mobile speakers. Their first product was a fold n' play speaker set using recycled materials and using zero external power. Their second product, "Rock-it" ($34.99) literally turns any device from a plastic cup to a cardboard box into a powerful mobile speaker. It is a product you have to see to believe.

How They're Doing It: OrigAudio was featured on ABC's Shark Tank where investors (including Marc Cuban) fought over the opportunity to invest. Jason and Mike eventually selected Robert Herjavec who offered a $150,000 investment for 15% of the company. However, before the show aired, OrigAudio's valuation quickly doubled and the founders tried to re-negotiate terms of the investment to protect the founder's equity. Robert and the duo were unable to lock in a successful deal.

That left the 2 founders as true Bootstrappers who have been able to fuel OrigAudio's growth from internal cash flow and found their success through successful PR, social media, word of mouth, and $0 spent on advertising. [187]

Sales have multiplied from $700,000 in 2010 to $2.5 million in 2011, and an expected cool $5 million in 2012. [187]

Where They Came From: University of California, Davis founders, Jason Lucash and Mike Syzmcak founded OrigAudio in 2009, during the heart of the economic recession. Three months after launching, their products were named one of Time magazine's 50 most innovative products.

After college, Mike and Jason found themselves on the road 200+ days a year working in corporate marketing for backpack maker, JanSport. The duo got tired of lugging around their portable

---

[187] http://www.entrepreneur.com/article/224256

speakers and batteries and thought they could build something better. [188]

The founders scraped together some savings and received a generous loan from Lucash's mom, giving the founders $30,000 to get OrigAudio off the ground. [188]

They leveraged their connections from JanSport and connected with a Chinese manufacturer to produce the company's first 6,000 speakers. Mike decided to quit his job and run the company full-time from his parents' house in Chicago while Mike continued to work full-time.[188]

OrigAudio received positive reviews from some magazines, but the company's big break thru came when Time magazine named OrigAudio's speakers as one of the Top 50 innovations of the year. A Time editor discovered OrigAudio from one of the airport kiosks that OrigAudio landed in.[188]

That initial media coverage launched OrigAudio into the national scene and have since distributed their products successfully through some of the nation's largest retailers.

---

[188] http://www.ocregister.com/articles/lucash-327250-origaudio-company.html

From $5,000 to $1 Billion—and Changing Women's Lives

Company: Spanx
Website: www.spanx.com
Last Known Revenue: $250 Million (2011)[189]

Who They Are: Spanx is a women's apparel company that began from an innovative pantyhose idea for women and has since expanded into more than 200 products.

How They're Doing It: Headquartered in Atlanta, GA, and opening retail shops across the United States, Spanx can now be found worldwide in more than 50 countries. In addition to "keeping butts covered" from Savannah to Singapore, Spanx also shapes the world by focusing on their mission: "To help women feel great about themselves and their potential."[190]

Where They Came From: Working as a sales trainer by day and performing stand-up comedy at night, founder Sara Blakely didn't know the first thing about the pantyhose industry—except that she dreaded wearing most pantyhose! But it wasn't until she couldn't find a thing to wear under a pair of white pants for a party that she took scissors, cut off the feet of those hose...and a new product was born.

She didn't start out to begin a business, just solve a wardrobe problem. However, it didn't take long of sharing what she'd done, and the nice-looking results, before Blakely thought her idea could become a real-life product for lots of other women. But she had no training in business; she'd never so much as taken a business course. As a result, she had only one source to operate from...her gut.

Blakely had an innovative idea and her life savings—$5,000[189]—to put behind it. But she knew if that idea wasn't going to get stolen out from under her, she'd need to patent it. She researched how to file a patent at the local library and wrote the patent herself, using a

---

[189] http://www.forbes.com/sites/clareoconnor/2012/03/07/undercover-billionaire-sara-blakely-joins-the-rich-list-thanks-to-spanx/
[190]
http://www.spanx.com/category/index.jsp?categoryId=4463905&clickId=topnav_aboutus_text

lawyer only to help write the claims. First step done and patent secured, she next looked to find a manufacturer to make the product. Due to her lack of financial security, however, most manufacturers didn't even look at her...until one, whose two daughters loved the product, decided to take the chance. She further differentiated the product with unique red packaging that featured three illustrated women on the front and the tagline, "Don't worry, we've got your butt covered!"[191]

Once Sara had her prototypes in hand, it was time to start selling. She called on Neiman Marcus, whose buyer agreed to meet with her—and showed her wares out of her "lucky red backpack." Three weeks later, Spanx was on the shelves of Neiman Marcus, and she knew she'd been handed a golden chance.[191]

"I then called all my friends," she says, "and begged them to go to Neiman's and make a huge fuss over the product and buy them up." She did the same thing with Saks, Nordstrom, Bloomingdales, and all other major retailers! Fortunately, at just the moment she was running out of friends, Spanx caught on, and the rest is history. [191]

It's one thing to catch on—it's another thing to maintain momentum for a new product. That generally takes advertising. Only problem? Blakely had no advertising budget. So what did she do?

"I hit the road," she says. "For the entire first year, I did in-store rallies about Spanx with the sales associates, and then stayed all day introducing customers to Spanx. I became notorious for lifting up my pant leg to every woman walking by." Her friends helped her call newspapers, magazines, and TV stations to get Spanx significant media coverage. [191]

Now, Spanx is a household word—in the media and in lives of women (and men!) everywhere. Blakely continues to be the sole owner of Spanx and has an estimated net worth of $1 billion,[192] making her one of the most envied women entrepreneurs in history.

But she's not sitting idle on that cash. Thanks to the Sara Blakely Foundation, organizations the world over help women better

---

[191] http://www.spanx.com/corp/index.jsp?page=sarasStory
[192] http://www.forbes.com/profile/sara-blakely/

themselves in countless ways. So, thanks to Spanx—women everywhere cannot only look good, but get a "leg up" on substantially improving their lives.

Now it's Your Turn

"It is not the critic who counts: not the man who points out how the strong man stumbles or where the doer of deeds could have done better. The credit belongs to the man who is actually in the arena, whose face is marred by dust and sweat and blood, who strives valiantly, who errs and comes up short again and again, because there is no effort without error or shortcoming, but who knows the great enthusiasms, the great devotions, who spends himself for a worthy cause; who, at the best, knows, in the end, the triumph of high achievement, and who, at the worst, if he fails, at least he fails while daring greatly, so that his place shall never be with those cold and timid souls who knew neither victory nor defeat." ~Theodore Roosevelt

You just read 75 amazing success stories of entrepreneurs that bootstrapped their startups to success. Many of the startups in Bootstrapped are still going strong. Others have been sold and the founders are on to new ventures.

The purpose of Bootstrapped is to show you that it's all possible. The only difference between the entrepreneurs in the book and you is one simple fact.

They have taken action to make things happen.

They overcame the same external and self- doubts that you yourself are facing. They faced the same challenges of not having a "good idea". Many of them didn't think they had enough money or enough time to successfully start their own business.

But guess what? They persevered through all of it. They are living proof that it can be done and that **you can do it, too!**

We live in an era where the barriers to starting your own profitable business have come crumbling down. The advent of the internet, crowdsourcing, social media, and more make it easier than ever to make great things happen without needing millions of dollars to get your idea off of the ground.

The point of Bootstrapped isn't to give you a week's worth of entertaining reading (although I certainly hope it did), **it is to get you to take action and to start your own business.**

The 75 startups and the entrepreneurs behind them show you how they achieved success and how you can achieve it, too. These entrepreneurs didn't have anything that you don't have right now!

So let's get started with your entrepreneurial journey and talk about the 4 things you need to get started with right now.

1.) Find a profitable business idea

This is where most aspiring entrepreneurs get stuck. They want to start their own business, but they just can't seem to find a "good" business idea.

Luckily for you, this is an easy fix. Thinking that you don't have a good idea is more self-doubt than anything else. In fact, the idea itself is only a small part of your key to success. Execution is far more important in building a successful startup.

Most startup ideas are bad ones. Ask your friends and family about your "great idea" and they'll tell you it's an awful idea...it will never succeed. All entrepreneurs face this external criticism which amplifies your internal fears and doubts.

This cumulative effect causes aspiring entrepreneurs to freeze. They get a good idea, get excited about it for a day or two and then the excitement fizzles. They find that others are "already doing" what they thought was original. Their friends and colleagues tell them that it is a bad idea. This is where most aspiring entrepreneurs stop.

Your job is to overcome the initial bombardment of self and external doubts and focus on moving your ideas forward. Don't freeze and stall when you tell yourself for the 5th time today that you no longer think your idea is a good one.

Before we put your cart before the horse though, let's take a look again at how some of the entrepreneurs in Bootstrapped came up with their profitable business ideas.

    a. **Scratch your own itch**
Frank Gruber and Eric Olson founded Tech Cocktail to scratch their own "itch" to meet and network with local entrepreneurs. What started as a small local gathering has now turned into a worldwide events and media company.

Take a look at the problems in your own life. Do you ever catch yourself saying, "I wish this were easier"? Sometimes, finding a great problem to solve will come from your own experiences and problems, but you need to be alert and observant of your own problems and brainstorm ways to resolve them.

    b. **Solve your friends and family's problems**

Kwame Kuadey founded Gift Card Rescue after hearing his friends complain about the gift cards they received to retailers that they didn't really like. Realizing the size of the problem and the number of gift cards bought and sold each year, he realized there could be an opportunity to leverage the internet to match buyers and sellers of unwanted gift cards.

Maybe you don't have any problems you think you can solve, but I guarantee your closest friends and family do. Aspiring entrepreneurs have keen ears and know how to "listen" for opportunities.

c. **Leverage your job experience and assess how you can better serve your own customers or solve a problem for your own company**
Prior to founding HubShout, Chad Hill led the marketing department for a startup and saw firsthand the struggle digital marketing agencies had with providing the analytics he sought. Hill thought he could do better and set out to prove it.

SurveyGizmo was started while the founders were working at MarketingSherpa and interviewed their own customers to identify unmet needs. It turns out that their unmet need was an easy way to survey their own customers. So the employees devised their idea for SurveyGizmo and were able to test their idea with their own customers without ever having to leave their jobs.

If you have an idea to make something better for your customers or your own company, this is often a clue to a great business idea. You can even incubate your idea internally to validate it before deciding to jump ship and pursue it full-time on your own.

Free resources to help you find a profitable business idea:

- Y-Combinator founder and startup guru, Paul Graham wrote a very insightful essay on how aspiring entrepreneurs can find a startup idea - http://paulgraham.com/startupideas.html
- Noah Kagan and team at AppSumo talk about how to use online analytics to find popular trends and ideas - http://www.fourhourworkweek.com/blog/2011/09/24/how-to-create-a-million-dollar-business-this-weekend-examples-appsumo-mint-chihuahuas/
- Idea Extraction is a technique used and taught by online entrepreneur Dane Maxwell - http://mixergy.com/dane-maxwell-foundation-interview/
- James Altucher, founder of StockPickr.com and renowned author, shows you how to come up with 10 business ideas every day - http://www.jamesaltucher.com/2012/10/how-to-become-an-idea-machine

2.) Optimize Your Idea

a.) Focus on a niche market first:

First time entrepreneurs get excited, and sometimes too excited. When they gain traction with their business, they want to open their business to everybody. But bootstrapping is about being profitable. And being profitable often means focusing on niche and premium markets first and then slowly expanding.

Slingshot SEO started out as a "general" internet marketing firm, but it wasn't until they realized they needed to focus on search engine optimization that they really started to grow and find their success.

Remember that even the biggest of businesses started somewhere. Starbucks started with a single store at

Pike Place in Seattle in 1971. Amazon started out only selling books, now they sell everything.

Do you remember the advice, Chad Hill, Hubshout founder had for aspiring entrepreneurs?

"Really identify your target market and your sales channel, because there is so much demand that it is hard to be a generalist."

Heed his advice and start small and focused.

b.) Create a sustainable business model

Having a "good" idea is just the start. Optimizing the details of your idea and turning it into a sustainable and profitable business are the keys to your success.

Steve Blank, entrepreneur and author of *The Four Steps to The Epiphany* and advocate for the "lean startup" movement, has numerous free resources online that show you how to take your "idea" and turn it into a viable business.

Free resources to help you create a viable business model:

- Business Model Canvas - http://steveblank.com/2010/10/25/entrepreneurship-as-a-science-%E2%80%93-the-business-modelcustomer-development-stack/
- Free e-course on entrepreneurship - https://www.udacity.com/course/ep245
- All of Steve's free material on entrepreneurship can be found here - http://steveblank.com/2012/11/27/open-source-entrepreneurship/

3.) Validate your idea

Many early stage entrepreneurs get overly excited when they think they have a great idea. What's the first thing they do? They go print business cards, incorporate their business, and spend money on "structuring" the business, rather than validating the business.

Validating your business is a way to mitigate the risks of a startup. It allows you to first see if there is actual demand for your product or service on a small scale before you invest any significant time or money on structuring your business.

Validating an idea can be as easy as selling your products on eBay or Craigslist. It could be setting up a website with a simple landing page asking people to sign-up once your product or service is available.

Free resources to help you validate your ideas:
- AppSumo's founder, Noah Kagan, has put together a great video on how to validate your business ideas over a weekend. There are 52 weekends in a year. If you take action now you can quickly test 50 or more ideas in the next year alone until you find one that will work - http://www.fourhourworkweek.com/blog/2011/09/24/how-to-create-a-million-dollar-business-this-weekend-examples-appsumo-mint-chihuahuas/
- A blog post on 3 quick ways to validate your business idea - http://www.bootstrappedbook.com/the-quickest-way-to-validate-your-business-ideas/

4.) Finance your startup

Many aspiring entrepreneurs convince themselves that they can't start their own business because they don't have enough money. Now that you've read Bootstrapped, you know that this is an excuse with numerous solutions.

Here are the five ways that bootstrappers were able to get enough money to not only start their businesses, but to sustain their livelihood while they were building their startups.

a) Consult in the same field as your startup

Aside from providing cash flow to cover your expenses, consulting is an opportunity to make connections and establish credibility in the same industry as your startup. Use your expertise as a consultant to network, build your client base and gain authority. All will be beneficial to building out your startup once you're ready to launch.

Look at Mike McDerment, founder of invoicing software FreshBooks. He worked as a full-time consultant as he built his software company on the side. Once FreshBooks became cash flow positive, McDerment was able to leave consulting behind and focus on building the company full-time.

b) Work a part-time job

Perhaps consulting isn't your thing, but you still need work just to keep the lights on. Your side job and your startup don't necessarily have to be related. Prioritize working on your startup during your most productive hours, and then take a part-time job on the side to make money. Whether it's tutoring or doing hourly manual labor, all sorts of jobs can give you the cushion you need to build your business during "non-working" hours.

Jason Ross, founder of JackThreads did exactly that. He worked as a bartender at night while building his online e-commerce business during the day.

c) Keep your full-time job

It's possible to stay put at your job and still move forward with your startup. You can use your position to learn valuable lessons that will pay dividends when you start your business. The key is to identify how you can take the initiative to teach yourself new skills, either at your job or on the side. If you're driven to succeed, you'll be able to make the most out of the resources you have available.

Sean Broihier, founder of FineArtAmerica.com, kept his job and still built his skill set on the side as an engineer in New York City. On top of his full-time position and launching his startup on the side, Sean also taught himself to write code.

d) Ask family members for a loan
Sometimes business and family don't mix, but then again, sometimes they do. It can be risky to borrow money, but if you are confident your startup will succeed, it can help get you up and running.

Mom and Dad have proven to be key supporters in some very successful entrepreneurs' lives. Jason Lucash and Mike Syzmcak, the founders of OrigAudio, borrowed money from Lucash's mom to help get their innovative startup off the ground. Now they're running a multi-million-dollar business and no longer have to rely on your parents.

e) Move in with your parents
Maybe Mom and Dad won't or can't offer you a loan, but they might give you a roof over your head. In fact, living with your parents after school has become the hot new trend; 85 percent of recent college grads move back in with their parents.[193]

Early on, Brendan Synnott and Kelly Flatley made this social sacrifice for their business. For 18 months, the founders of Bear Naked granola worked out of their parents' homes with no income. The company's first office space was a spare bedroom in Kelly's parents' house. Later, they sold their company to Kellogg for $60 million.

---

[193] http://newsfeed.time.com/2011/05/10/survey-85-of-new-college-grads-moving-back-in-with-mom-and-dad/

So what's your next step?

TAKE ACTION.

Stop telling yourself you don't have any good ideas. Write some ideas down. Go test them. Don't tell yourself you can't afford it. Get creative.

There are 75 examples in Bootstrapped that show you how entrepreneurs came up with their business ideas, grew their business, and financed their startups.

Use these case studies to stimulate your own business ideas and to find creative ways around the barriers that are preventing you from building something great.

So put this book down now, you're at the end anyway. Seriously, **RIGHT NOW and get started.**